THE WITCH'S PATH

© Brittany Little

About the Author

Thorn Mooney is a Witch of more than twenty years and the high priestess of Foxfire, a traditional Gardnerian coven thriving in the American South. She holds graduate degrees in religious studies and English literature and has worked as a university lecturer, public school teacher, academic journal manager, tarot reader, writer, and musician. Thorn maintains a long-standing YouTube channel, has been blogging about Witchcraft and the occult for more than a decade, and is a regular at Pagan festivals throughout the United States. She lives in Raleigh, North Carolina. Follow her on Instagram at @thornthewitch and read more at www.thornthewitch.com.

THE WITCH'S PATH

Advancing Your Craft at Every Level

THORN MOONEY

Llewellyn Publications
Woodbury, Minnesota

FIRST EDITION
Second Printing, 2021

Cover design by Shira Atakpu
Cover illustration by Jessica Roux / Stonesong Press, LLC

Llewellyn Publications is a registered trademark of Llewellyn Worldwide Ltd.

Library of Congress Cataloging-in-Publication Data
Names: Mooney, Thorn, author.
Title: The witch's path : advancing your path at every level / Thorn
   Mooney.
Description: First edition. | Woodbury, Minnesota : Llewellyn Publications,
   2021. | Includes bibliographical references. | Summary: "This book
   explores the most common themes a witch may explore to work their way
   out of a rut: sacred space, devotion, ritual and magic, personal
   practice, and community. Mooney offers exercises and techniques to renew
   your sense of engagement and move forward spiritually"— Provided by
   publisher.
Identifiers: LCCN 2021019246 (print) | LCCN 2021019247 (ebook) | ISBN
   9780738763774 (paperback) | ISBN 9780738764108 (ebook)
Subjects: LCSH: Witchcraft.
Classification: LCC BF1566 .M68 2021 (print) | LCC BF1566 (ebook) | DDC
   133.4/3—dc23
LC record available at https://lccn.loc.gov/2021019246
LC ebook record available at https://lccn.loc.gov/2021019247

Llewellyn Worldwide Ltd. does not participate in, endorse, or have any authority or responsibility concerning private business transactions between our authors and the public.

All mail addressed to the author is forwarded but the publisher cannot, unless specifically instructed by the author, give out an address or phone number.

Any internet references contained in this work are current at publication time, but the publisher cannot guarantee that a specific location will continue to be maintained. Please refer to the publisher's website for links to authors' websites and other sources.

Llewellyn Publications
A Division of Llewellyn Worldwide Ltd.
2143 Wooddale Drive
Woodbury, MN 55125-2989
www.llewellyn.com

Printed in the United States of America

Also by Thorn Mooney

Traditional Wicca: A Seeker's Guide

For Corvus

Contents

Acknowledgments

Second books, it turns out, can be a lot harder than first books. *Traditional Wicca* came with relative ease and sort of sprung to life fully formed. This book, however, had to be pulled out in chunks, turned over, rewritten, thrown out, and then assembled into something that would serve a much larger group of seekers and practitioners. I wrote it when I was myself on a plateau, dealing with burnout and frustration. Good for generating insight—not so good for steady, consistent writing. But there were lots of people to help me along the way.

To Corvus, for phone calls and coffee and the deepest of deep Soul Asylum songs. Readers, if you see Corvus around online or at a festival, share your cat pictures and tell her she's great. None of this would happen without her.

To Matt, because, like that charming cowboy cop in *Practical Magic*, I was pretty sure you didn't exist. I'm so thrilled every day that you do.

To Jason Mankey, for encouraging me to write books and always being an ear. And to Ari Mankey for mixing the best cocktails, plotting our shared adventures, and being the sort of high priestess we should all hope to be.

To Kelden, for being my writing buddy and letting me vent while I was in book jail. Let's go back to school and stop with all of this author nonsense.

To Christopher Penczak and all my mentors and friends with the Temple of Witchcraft, especially Julia, Tessa, Deryn, Abigail, and Tina Marie. I'm so grateful to have you all in my life!

To Kithic, for being a source of great ideas and true camaraderie. I'm pretty sure you're the smartest bunch of Witches, Pagans, and magicians on the internet. I'm so glad to have found you. Big shout-outs to Rhi, Maewyn, and Veles who are actual geniuses. Maewyn, I'm so glad we circled back into each other's lives. Rhi, you are one of the wisest people I know. I'm so glad you're not a nun. Veles, we're going to ambush you one day. Thank you for the years of friendship. Hugs, high fives, and late-night drinks to Spoons, Salt, Thorn, A. Llewellyn, Michael, Matt, Frank, Azaizall, Wren, and the rest of Amyranth.

To Foxfire, as always. Thank you for the years of magic and for helping me to figure all this out. Sorry it gets messy sometimes. I'm so proud of you. Here, have these matches. I'm so excited for whatever comes next.

And, finally, to the covenleaders and teachers who've taught me what I learned along the way and the friends who've allowed me to share their stories. I'm not really that smart, everybody; I've just surrounded myself with smart people who have a better handle on things than I do and are kind enough to let me write about them.

Introduction

It's a full moon tonight. I gaze out my kitchen window, watching dark clouds roll across the night sky. It's too bright to see the stars. Online they're calling it a "super moon," because it's closer to Earth in its orbit than usual, which makes it appear particularly large. This combined with gently swaying poplars and crickets chirruping in the summer air makes for a picturesque backdrop to any television-worthy Witchcraft ritual.

There was a time in my life, particularly toward the beginning of my practice of the Craft, when I would have planned an elaborate working to mark the occasion. The full moon is a great time to work magic, and I would have taken advantage of the opportunity. Maybe a spell for wealth or luck. Maybe I would have written a meditation and blended an appropriate incense to encourage visions. Maybe I would have cleansed and reconsecrated my altar and simply sat in silent prayer.

But not tonight. I had a long day at work and have a lot of other things on my mind. My boss is driving me nuts, I'm worried that I've mis-budgeted and won't have enough money to pay the car repair bill I just received, and I still need to figure out what weekend would be good for our next coven meeting. I try to schedule two per month, but between a full-time job, birthdays, illnesses, and travel, it's more like once per month. I'm exhausted, and I just want to sit on my couch with a glass of wine and the remote control. That would be okay every now and then, but the truth is that I've made a bit of a habit out of this. This isn't the first full moon I've skipped.

I flop on the couch and reach for my datebook, which I maintain fervently. I have to, or my whole life would fall apart. In all the chaos of last month, I missed the summer solstice. I organized a ritual for some of my covenmates and spent the day at a festival with my local Pagan community, but I didn't take the time to do something to mark the season in a personal way. Those two events were fun, but they were more for others than me. My job as the high priestess of my coven is to teach my tradition to others and to model effective ritual for my students. My personal spiritual growth and relationship with our gods is a part of that (that's how I got here in the first place), but my obligations to others are the priority. The festival was fun, but I was there as a presenter. Functionally, I was there to work, not to celebrate. So even though I did things for the solstice, I didn't necessarily do things that fed my *own* Craft and nurtured my *own* spirit.

After months of this, I'm starting to feel it. No wonder I feel so disconnected these days! I've been working as a priestess, but I haven't been doing it in such a way that refuels me. I'm speaking and writing for Pagan communities, but I've been neglecting my own spiritual needs. I'm a covenleader and a high priestess, but somewhere along the way I stopped being a Witch. I didn't even know that was possible.

It's time to just admit it: I've fallen into a magical rut. I'm not sure exactly when it happened, but I recognize the feeling because, after more than twenty years of practicing Witchcraft, I've been here before.

Hitting the Wall

I discovered Wicca in my early teens, inspired, like many, by movies and television shows. I devoured books and websites (it was the late nineties, so there weren't as many of the latter), learning as much as I could, as fast as I could. I discovered the great variety of Witchcrafts in the world—Wicca was only one side of a long and intricate story. I explored as many as I could. I met others, got involved in several different Pagan and Witch communities, and ultimately joined a coven in the Gardnerian tradition and became a high priestess in my own right. Social media opened up countless ways to meet and learn from Witches and other types of magicians all over the world. There are now thousands of books to choose from and specialty retailers that cater to Witches, both online and off, based in towns and cities all over the world. It's easier than it's ever been to develop as a Witch.

But sometimes things just don't go that smoothly.

As blessed as my life has been, there have been points in my path as a Witch where I have felt stuck. Stagnant. Unsure of where to go next. Most recently, that happened as a covenleader. I had spent so much time turning my spirituality into my job that I'd lost the magic of it all, which is how I ended up on that couch ignoring a gorgeous full moon to watch TV and sulk. Years before that, I'd been a seeker, with more book knowledge than experience, frustrated in my search for "advanced" books and teachers who could take me beyond what I'd already been doing on my own. I was lucky enough to find a coven and a tradition that helped push me out of that rut, but many Witches don't have access to those kinds of opportunities, or else they prefer to remain solitary (and, by the way, being in a coven doesn't mean you won't experience stagnation).

And then there was my very first hurdle as a Witch: getting started! I remember discovering Witchcraft and borrowing my first books and falling in love. I felt like my whole world was blown open in an instant. There was so much to learn and try. Where to even start? How would I know if I was doing it right? How would I find guidance in the midst of so much misinformation? It ended up taking months to work up the courage to try my first rituals and to begin building a personal practice.

When you first begin exploring Witchcraft, life feels almost overwhelmingly magical. From the outside, it's easy to think that Witches are ethereal people who spend their days glorifying the beauty of nature, harnessing arcane powers, and building meaningful ritual into every mundane activity, but the truth is that we're all still just human beings. We have stressful jobs and car payments and family drama and days when we just don't feel very magical. Sometimes life gets so crazy that we put our spirituality on the backburner.

Finding yourself on a magical plateau is actually a common experience, though the particular challenges we face at any given time may be different. You may be trying to negotiate how to fit a Craft practice into your chaotic daily schedule. On the other hand, you may have all the time in the world but are so bogged down by new information and magical theory that you don't know how to begin applying it. In wider Pagan and Witch communities, you'll sometimes hear people talk about the "armchair occultist"—a person who has a lot of book knowledge but doesn't actually *do* anything with it. It's common for both beginning and advanced practitioners to find themselves in this position. Just like burnout and exhaustion, these can leave us stuck on magical and spiritual plateaus. Though these scenarios are different, the fundamental question in each case is the same: Where do I go next?

How to Use This Book

This book was born out of those bumps that arise throughout a Witch's life, and it's suitable for all but the most absolute of beginners (i.e., I won't spend much time on basic vocabulary or endlessly list all the types of Witchcraft you might choose from). What do you do in those moments when you feel stuck, lost, burned out, or just unsure of how to take that next step? How do you revive a lagging practice or kick-start a new one? How do you harness (or recapture) the magic in your life? Wherever you find yourself in this moment—overwhelmed budding Witch, disillusioned adept, jaded covenleader, or anywhere in between—how do you take your Witchcraft to the next level? If you've never even tried to cast a spell before, but you've been dying to try and already think of yourself as a Witch in your heart, this book is as much for you as anyone. If you've been running a coven for years but still feel like you need encouragement and a fresh perspective, this book is for you too.

Together we'll look at some of the most important and most common aspects of Witchcraft, whatever your particular style or tradition. We'll reconsider certain practices, like creating sacred space and performing ritual, that sometimes get taken for granted or even go totally unexplained or unexamined in popular conversation. We'll also tackle topics that sometimes feel so complicated that they leave people wondering where to start, like interacting with gods or spirits and building meaningful ritual. Each chapter is full of ideas to help you expand your practice, reevaluate your thinking, and inspire you to move forward as a Witch. I've also shared my experiences struggling at various points in my own Craft.

At the end of each chapter is a structured activity, with modifications based on one of the four Classical elements that serve as the cornerstones to many types of Witchcraft: Air, Fire, Water, and Earth. Are you a beginner looking to take your first steps? Look to Air, the element of beginnings, the dawn, and the awakening of a new way of thinking. Are you an advanced practitioner trying to shake up the routine? Consider Water, to go deeper, to uncover further mysteries, and to expand your experience. Are you just looking for easy ways to incorporate your Witchcraft into a crowded schedule and build a routine? Fire will teach you quickness, efficiency, and an appreciation for getting straight to the point. Or are you dealing with burnout? Earth asks you to reconsider your foundations and examine what lies at the root of your practice.

No matter where you are, you'll find strategies for jump-starting your Craft practice. You may be at different places depending on the subject—a novice at working with the gods (if you even believe in them—and it's fine if you don't!) but an old hand at spellcasting. Pick and choose as suits your needs, but don't treat these activities as optional. They are designed to push you to action, and that requires that you actually get up and *do* something. You should feel challenged but not overwhelmed, so choose accordingly. Where possible, I've also provided alternatives to visualization and lengthy periods spent in sitting meditation, to accommodate Witches with aphantasia, ADHD, and other cognitive needs that make such activities either unnecessarily difficult or even impossible. There are many ways to be a Witch and practice magic, and I welcome you to modify the exercises in each chapter to suit your own unique situations.

I've written this book so that you can skip around as you like, but if you read from beginning to end, you'll notice that I've started with topics that are foundational, individual, and largely private. I then move to subjects that are more complex and potentially entail larger communities. We start with the most basic assumptions about what it means to be a Witch, what Witchcraft is for, and how our personal definitions (which so often change over time) impact our practice. From there, we explore personal sacred space, devotion and working with entities other than ourselves, and then ritual and magic. We end with considerations of our interactions with others, moving into wider communities (whether online or off), and building plans for continuing to move forward to a stronger personal practice.

If some of these things sound simple, it's because they are! But in order to build a strong, meaningful practice of the Craft, we have to consider its most basic structures and tenets, even if we think we've already seen it all. Sometimes, next-level practice comes out of reconsidering those things we stopped looking at ages ago. If our foundations are weak, crumbling, or just straining from too much weight, we need to rebuild and reinforce them.

Please note that I have chosen to capitalize *Witch* and *Witchcraft* throughout this book. This is largely for the sake of simplicity. Many Witches choose to capitalize the word when referring to religious traditions of Witchcraft but to leave it lowercase when discussing historical cases of Witchcraft or non-religious contemporary traditions. This practice, however, becomes overly complicated, especially when we add the abbreviation *Craft*, which is frequently capitalized even despite the above convention. Because I am discussing many types of Witchcraft, I chose to simplify and to provide specific context where necessary. Do not take this to mean that all Witches are practicing a single tradition, or that those persecuted as Witches throughout history are inherently related to contemporary Witches. Additionally, I do not use *Wicca* and *Witchcraft* interchangeably. Wicca is a type of Witchcraft and Wiccans are Witches, but where I am referring to Wicca, I will do so directly so as to avoid confusion. Where necessary, I also distinguish between eclectic forms of Wicca and traditional initiatory Wicca. Similarly, please note that *god* and *goddess* are presented in lowercase unless they explicitly refer to *the God* or *the Goddess* as formal titles for Wiccan deities, whose names are generally regarded to be either secret or else unnecessary, as some Wiccan traditions teach that they encompass all gods and goddesses, according to specific interpretations. I respect this convention where appropriate, but do not conflate it with the great variety of languages that other types of Witches use to discuss the divine. There are no agreed-upon standards, even among Witches of the same tradition.

In any practice of Witchcraft, it's normal to fall into a funk from time to time. We hit walls, life gets in the way, and we periodically have to recalibrate our beliefs and practices as we grow and change in other parts of our lives. My Craft doesn't look the same as it did when I first started, and yours probably doesn't either. If you're new to Witchcraft, you're *already* in the midst of big changes in your life. Dealing with change and pushing forward is part of the work of the Witch. It can be difficult but also a lot of fun. Enjoy the experience!

Chapter 1
What Exactly Is Witchcraft?

Across history, the Witch enchants us. Benevolent or wicked, youthful or haggard, man, woman, or someone (or something!) that defies such simple categorization, Witches have thrived throughout Western culture. They serve as both villains and heroes in favorite stories, as points of controversy and violence in history, and as inspiration in our personal spiritual explorations. We love them, we're afraid of them, and, for an increasing many, we are them. Given that the Witch is such a complex figure, it's no surprise that Witches generate so much confusion: What exactly makes someone a Witch? How does a person become one? Why would someone want to? What types of Witchcraft exist, and what makes them all distinct? What does a practice of Witchcraft actually require and entail?

We humans love rules and categories. We feel compelled to sort and label things, and that leads to lots of absolute statements about what things are and how we should talk about them. If you just went by today's internet hashtags, you might think a Witch is a young, hip woman (and only a woman) with an interest in tarot cards and a massive crystal collection. She does yoga, has a perfect manicure, and is very interested in holistic healing. Before that, back when I was first learning about Witchcraft in the nineties, Witchcraft and Wicca were used interchangeably. A cursory glance through books from that era reveals a Witch who adheres strictly to the rule of "harm none" and worships a triple goddess in the form of Maiden, Mother, and Crone. All gods and goddesses are really aspects of one God and Goddess. Witches were never dark, never practiced baneful magic, and were very adamantly practicing a religion.

But let's go back even further! Just a few decades earlier, before *Wicca* was a term everyone knew, we had the Witch Cult. Contemporary Witches met in secretive covens and were said to be practicing a surviving magical tradition indigenous to the British Isles. To be a Witch, you had to be formally initiated and taught the sacred names of the gods and the working of the rites. The exact goings-on of coven life were a secret, at least until writers like Gerald Gardner, Doreen Valiente, Justine Glass, Lois Bourne, Stewart Farrar, and many others began sharing material with the public. Even before this, Witchcraft has been a family tradition, rooted in the folklore of the lands that birthed it, varying by region. And all along the way, Witchcraft has been a Christian heresy, the path of the Devil, and at times a crime punishable by death.

So which of these is really Witchcraft? Which should be our standard?

The truth is that we don't agree on any single definition of Witchcraft or on the exact nature of the Witch. That's why there's so much variety! All the above are types of Witches, even where they contradict one another. Furthermore, most of these types of Witches have existed at the same time. I've long since given up trying to come up with a single definition that will apply equally well to all times, cultures, and individuals. This usually just creates big headaches and anger, and I'm not convinced that it's all that useful an endeavor. Who and what a Witch is and what we think Witchcraft can do seems to depend more on who we are, what time period we occupy, and in what region we are than anything inherent or objective about Witches. Instead, I prefer a pragmatic approach. Our real concern is our own practice, our own traditions, and our own communities. Others are free to construct their own definitions and boundaries as they see fit.

For the purposes of this book, let's consider some of the things that these different types of Witchcraft have in common. After all, just because we probably can't come up with a definition that satisfies everyone, that doesn't mean you shouldn't know damn well what Witchcraft is for *you*. If you're new to the Craft, some of this may be surprising—it often flies in the face of more popularly circulated ideas about what Witchcraft is (especially if your background is in contemporary eclectic forms of Wicca). If you're a more seasoned Witch, this chapter is still worth your time. Sometimes, the walls we hit in our own practice come out of long-standing assumptions about what it is that we're doing. If your perspectives about what Witchcraft is, what it's for, and what it can do haven't changed since you first began practicing, then it can be valuable to reconsider things. If you arrive at the same conclusions, then your convictions will be stronger for it. If you discover something new or change your mind about something, then you'll have new avenues to explore. In either case, your own Craft will be reinvigorated.

Crossing Boundaries

There's a reason why Witches in fairy tales, fantasy novels, and horror movies are frequently villains. No matter how much good press contemporary Witches earn or how many times you yourself may insist to friends and acquaintances that you are practicing a life-affirming religion, that you don't worship Satan, that you don't practice baneful magic, that you strive for balance and harmony with nature—or whatever your go-to defense of your Craft to outsiders has been—it just doesn't seem to sink in for most people. Aside from the fact that none of us can speak to what all Witches do or don't do (some *are*, in fact, Satanists, many do practice baneful magic, and, increasingly, some do *not* consider what they do a religion), Witchcraft has a long and tangled history and the idea that Witches are automatically bad guys in the story isn't going to be undone in just a few decades.

In fact, when we sit down and consider most of the storybook Witches we grew up with, it's hard not to wonder if maybe *we're* the ones who have it wrong. They are, after all, usually, inarguably, villains. In the early twentieth century, folklorist Margaret Murray (1863–1963) concluded that the reason for this was conscious effort on the part of the various Christian churches taking control of Western Europe for more than a thousand years. Witches, according to Murray, were practitioners of a pre-Christian religion indigenous to Europe, centered upon the worship of a horned god of the hunt surviving from the Paleolithic era.[1] That Witches ended up being constantly cast in the role of the antagonist was the result of a consciously orchestrated campaign on the part of Christian leaders seeking to justify exterminating their religious rivals. It's a lot easier to murder and oppress people if you first turn them into villains.

Margaret Murray's ideas are no longer accepted by scholars today, but they held sway for decades, and continue to inspire contemporary Witches long after being discredited. If you've ever insisted that Witchcraft is rooted in ancient religious practice or that the horned god of the hunt and the goddess of the moon have survived in various forms throughout Europe, then Margaret Murray deserves a tip of your hat, even if you've never read her books.

It bothered Murray, as it bothers many of us, that Witches get such a bad rap. Arguably, one of the reasons why Gerald Gardner—Wicca's famed founder—came to emphasize his own practice as "white witchcraft" and why the so-called Wiccan Rede—"An it harm none, do as ye will"—came to have so much prominence as Wicca developed was because Witches of the day were so invested in changing popular perceptions. Until very recently, Witchcraft was illegal in England, so it made sense for the Witches at that time to work so hard to represent themselves as gentle and harmless, even if the real story was somewhat more complicated.

Nonetheless, stories about evil, scary Witches continue. Even in stories where Witches are positive characters, they often have darker, less friendly kin. J. K. Rowling's Harry Potter franchise is the most obvious contemporary example in which we see Witches as both heroes and villains. Consider further benevolent Cordelia Foxx versus power-hungry Fiona Goode in *American Horror Story: Coven*, or the conflict between light Witches and dark in Kami Garcia and Margaret Stohl's popular young adult novel *Beautiful Creatures*. In Cate Tiernan's *Sweep* series, teen Witch Morgan Rowlands wonders if she can ever truly be good, despite being born to a dark clan of hereditary Witches. Look at kind-hearted Sabrina Spellman versus the conniving Weird Sisters in Netflix's *Chilling Adventures of Sabrina*. In all these narratives, we have young Witches choosing

---

1. Margaret Murray, *The God of the Witches* (New York: Oxford University Press, 1952).

sides. In our contemporary storytelling, at the very least we now believe that Witches can be both: good and evil, light and dark.

Historically, both in imagination and in truth, Witches have been "others." Good or evil, they are distinct from "normal" people because of the power they possess. They are either hated for it and hunted down, or sought out fearfully in times of great need. Even when they work their magic for good, Witches are scary. They exist outside of society, whether literally (as when they make their homes outside the village walls) or figuratively (as in the case of the wealthy Witch in the imposing house everyone passes on their daily rounds and whispers about in private). Whatever flavor of Witchcraft we consider, the idea that the Witch is an outsider persists. Even when they seek to be included in everyday society (like Sally Owens in *Practical Magic*, Samantha Stephens in *Bewitched*, or Prue Halliwell in *Charmed*), their differences are impossible to hide.

So what does that mean for us as contemporary Witches?

I'd like to suggest that we embrace that identity. Being on the outside of something allows for a unique perspective. It creates the space to notice patterns and then to affect them where necessary. It also places us closer to other worlds, other ways of being. One of the hallmarks of Witchcraft is the ability to traverse other realms, whether that means the spirit realm, the underworld, hell, or the dark forest beyond the village. Wiccans talk about operating "between the worlds," usually in the form of a magic circle. Traditional Witches speak of "hedgecrossing." Still more types of Witches describe journeying to "the astral." Witches can do all these things because they're already one step closer to these outside spaces than other people.

In recent years—and especially for Witches with eclectic Wiccan and New Age backgrounds—it's become customary (even perfunctory) to insist that we *aren't* different. That we're misunderstood, that we're practicing a religion like any other, and that people shouldn't fear or avoid us. These efforts have a time and a place. There have been plenty of points in history when it would have been in your best interest to hide your Craft. Many of us continue to have to hide, from conservative family members, employers and coworkers, and others. That's true. Your safety is always paramount, and it shouldn't be disregarded casually. But for an increasing number of us, we *can* be open, especially if we otherwise occupy positions of privilege.[2] And even if we're not directly telling people that we're Witches (call me old-fashioned, but I don't think your boss *ever* needs to know about your personal life, especially your religion or your politics), they often still have a sense that we're different. More observant, perhaps, or more introspective. More outspoken. More creative. Bolder. But there's no need for anyone to know *why* you are the way you are unless you wish to share.

When we're conscious of our difference and we embrace it gleefully, it lends us even more power. Think of the people in your life you admire the most. Think of the great thinkers, builders, artists, and activists of history. Chances are, whoever came to mind first was at one time viewed as an outlier, a weirdo, a rabble-rouser, or even crazy. In short, dangerous. Great change and great power rarely come from a place of normalcy. If your Witchcraft isn't setting you apart in some way, I would, frankly, question its effectiveness.

As a Witch, I may not live on the edge of a forest and I may not eat children or curse my neighbors' cattle, but I *am* scary. I *am* an outsider. I'm scary because I see the status quo and I question it. I speak out against the dominant powers and leading modes of thought where I see injustice, inefficiency, cruelty, or oppression. I seek to empower those around me. I am working to change my reality for the better, and that sometimes means working against the powers that be. I seek to change *myself.* I deny the power of cruel gods and unjust religious institutions and hierarchies. I value freedom. And I've cultivated the magical power to change the world as I see fit, without begging permission or offering explanation.

I don't need to hide in the woods to be terrifying.

So, no, I am *not* normal. If you're reading this, there's a better than fair chance that you're not either. In this way, Witchcraft, though it is many things to many people, is traceable and recognizable.

Witches are scary. Period.

---

2. Consider, for example, that so many of us still enjoy white, heterosexual, cisgender privilege. We may be religious "others" (even when we don't identify as religious), but we are rarely targets for the violence, discrimination, and exclusion experienced by people of color, queer people, and others whose "otherness" is impossible to hide.

Making Magic

Even more central to Witchcraft than suspicion, fear, and transgression, is magic. Witches are magic workers. In stories, in history, and in pop culture, Witches are Witches because they possess powers beyond those of regular people. These powers vary. Witches in medieval European trial records could render men impotent, fly through the air, and spread sickness. Witches in fairy tales can often communicate with animals or even transform into them. They can make people fall in love, grant wishes, and make whole kingdoms crumble. Today's Witches claim to be able to heal with herbal potions and burning candles; to travel in astral realms; to tell the future in cards, stars, and tea leaves; and even to speak directly with gods and spirits.

These are all incredible things. If we were only capable of *some* of this, we would be up to something truly remarkable. But is all of this really possible? And even if it is, what about all of the other kinds of magic in the world? How is Witchcraft distinct from ceremonial magic, Hoodoo, Christian gifts of the Holy Spirit, prayer, Reiki, herbalism, or any of the countless other practices in the world that could be construed as magical? Even Witches sometimes insist that spells are no different than prayers or that other magical traditions (like Southern American folk magic, for example) are really just Witchcraft by other names. So what's the deal? How do we define and consider the magic practiced uniquely by Witches?

There's a good chance you've already heard that Witches spell magic with a *K* to distinguish it from stage magic. This practice really took hold in the eighties and nineties thanks to a publishing boom and particularly the widespread influence of Wiccan authors like Raymond Buckland, Silver RavenWolf, Christopher Penczak, and DJ Conway. It's worth noting, however, that this practice isn't even actually Wiccan, because we don't see it in Wiccan books before then (and it's particularly noteworthy that we don't see it from Wicca's earliest writers, Gerald Gardner and Doreen Valiente). We also don't see *magick* used by other kinds of Witches, like those inspired by Robert Cochrane, Cecil Williamson, and more contemporary writers like Gemma Gary and Robin Artisson.

Aleister Crowley (1875–1947), the famed twentieth-century magician and leader of the Ordo Templi Orientis, usually gets the credit for adding the *K* to magic to consciously distinguish it. The *K* wasn't just to keep people from being confused (and, come on, do people *really* mistake what contemporary Witches do for what David Copperfield does in Las Vegas?). Rather, magick for Crowley was the method by which an individual could come to acquire self-understanding and thereby the power to exercise one's true Will. This goes beyond simple wants and needs but instead refers to the attainment of one's destiny. Ceremonial magicians and others sometimes refer to this sort of magic as "high magic," with the practices of Witches, folk magicians, and others being "low magic," because low magic is generally more concerned with mundane issues like physical health, finding or keeping love, being hired for jobs, and the like. Changing the spelling was a way to differentiate high magic—magic concerning one's higher self—with low (for this reason, perhaps Witches really *shouldn't* use the *K*). Crowley had other more sophisticated reasons for adding the *K* too, particularly pertaining to numerological associations with the numbers 6 (the number of letters in *magick*) and 11 (*K* is the eleventh letter of the alphabet). Over the years, the *K* has stuck, particularly in ceremonial spaces and in eclectic Wiccan spaces.[3]

Aleister Crowley and his contemporaries and followers did not (and overwhelmingly *do* not) consider themselves Witches. Nor do most root doctors, faith healers, shamans, or Spiritualist mediums. Thanks to colonialism, globalization, wanton mass publishing, and the internet, there's a tendency for many contemporary Witches to think of all magical, spiritual practices as somehow being the same, or at least related. We see a Vodou priestess making offerings to the spirits and we liken it to our own devotional work. We see Spiritualist churches employing séances to speak with the dead and we recognize it as necromancy. We love throwing around the word *shaman* too, thanks in large part to New Age appropriations. Even Scott Cunningham, that most beloved Wiccan author, opens his bestseller *Wicca: A Guide for the Solitary Practitioner* with the insistence

---

3. For more, consider Aleister Crowley's essay "The Revival of Magick," available as part of a collection by the same name from New Falcon Publications, edited by Hymenaeus Beta and Richard Kaczynski.

that "many of the techniques of Wicca are shamanic in origin."[4] Many Witches also insist that their Craft is connected to Eastern religion (as though that by itself is a singular thing) and therefore incorporate yoga, chakra healing, and conceptions of karma.

There's lots of room here to conflate Witchcraft with other traditions and practices. Some of these are reasonable and harmless, but others potentially do great damage to marginalized groups and religions and should be approached carefully or avoided altogether. It's tempting to point to only certain kinds of Witchcraft and particularly blatant examples, but cultural appropriation is a problem that impacts all kinds of Witches. You'll have to do your homework and use your best judgment here, but I bring it up now because it's useful in laying the groundwork for what we mean by "magic" in a discussion of Witchcraft.

Rather than landing on one extreme and arguing that *all* magic is really Witchcraft, and instead of falling back on the dichotomy of high magic (or magick, if you prefer) and low magic, I prefer to nuance things by turning to psychologist Abraham Maslow (1908–1970). Maslow is most famous for his hierarchy of needs, which he first described in the journal *Psychological Review* in 1943. This hierarchy of needs is still used by psychologists and social scientists today to explain what motivates people to behave in particular ways, and it suggests that we can't tend to some needs without first meeting others. At the bottom of the hierarchy (you can imagine a pyramid, as this is frequently how Maslow's hierarchy of needs is illustrated) are foundational, physiological needs: food, shelter, sleep, sex, and the like. Above that we find security: health, financial stability, emotional security, and so on. This progresses to social belonging—the need for friendship and intimacy. The final tiers are esteem and self-actualization, with self-actualization sitting at the very top of the pyramid. Esteem includes the need for self-respect, self-confidence, independence, and a sense of personal freedom. Self-actualization, that elusive pinnacle of human experience, includes more abstract needs, like seeking

---

4. Scott Cunningham, *Wicca: A Guide for the Solitary Practitioner* (Woodbury, MN: Llewellyn Publications, 1990), 4.

happiness, fulfilling one's destiny, and developing personal talent for the sake of it.[5]

There have been many revisions and much reframing of Maslow's hierarchy of needs over the years, but it's safe to say that we start with our most basic needs and move on as those needs are met. We operate in different places at different times in life, and where we fall is closely tied to economic class, the bodies we were born into, and the cultures that raised us.

Throughout history and in storytelling across the ages, the magic practiced by Witches tends to operate on the lower and middle rungs of the hierarchy. People go to Witches to cure illness, to find lovers, to secure jobs, to win court battles, and to protect loved ones from harm. There's a reason why most spell books on the shelves today revolve around money, love, and healing. This is also why many Witches choose to practice outside the realm of any religion or devotional tradition. Working magic doesn't necessarily have anything to do with gods! It's also why it's not always fair to equate casting a spell with praying.

Where Witches *are* interested in self-actualization, ascension (as some traditions call it), and personal development, it's often thanks to the influence of other magical groups and religious practices. Wicca, for example, was born in the midst of a European occult revival and has close ties to the magical order of the Golden Dawn, Hermeticism, and the works of non-Witches like Aleister Crowley and Dion Fortune. Today's Witches are also heavily influenced by the American New Age movement, Theosophy, New Thought, and Western European interpretations of Buddhism, from which we pull things like crystal healing, ascended masters, Zen meditation, karma, and reincarnation.

You'll see a mix of magical concepts discussed in this book, and I will do my best to note their origins, as well as their practical applications. Your task moving forward is to consider your own magical practice. Where on the hierarchy does it fall? What is it that you would *like* to focus on and be able to do? How is it that your magic is Witchcraft rather than something else?

---

5. You can read more in Abraham Maslow's *Motivation and Personality*, first published by Harper (now HarperCollins) in 1954.

Working with Spirits

In "Snow White," the evil queen uses a magic mirror to carry out her murderous plans. She isn't simply scrying for signs and omens; she actually speaks to the spirit of the mirror directly, and it provides her with knowledge that she could not achieve on her own. In some versions of the story, the magic mirror has greater or lesser degrees of agency. Sometimes it is cold and placid, like an impersonal Magic 8-Ball. Other times it jeers and cracks jokes and even cries when the evil queen threatens to break it. The mirror isn't a god or an ancestral spirit, and the evil queen certainly doesn't worship or serve the mirror. It serves her, though most versions of the story don't tell us why.

The magic mirror in Snow White is a solid example of what many might recognize as a familiar—a spirit that does the Witch's bidding. Throughout history, familiar spirits have been understood as non-corporeal entities summoned or even created by the Witch, or sometimes spirits and demons who take the form of animals as necessary. Toads, rabbits, cats, goats, and dogs—the sorts of creatures you could find easily on a Western European or American colonial farm—were all common choices, and on rare occasions during the Witch hunts, actual animals were executed as Witches.[6] Additionally, one of the ways to convict a suspected Witch was to strip her naked and examine her body for a "Witch's mark" (which could be a mole, a birthmark, a scar, or even just a patch of skin that supposedly didn't register pain), where familiars were thought to suckle. All Witch hunters knew that Witches work with spirits, so that's what they looked for.

And not just familiars! Witches were just as likely to work with devils, demons, faeries, and the shades of the dead. They may not have these spirits bound to them like familiars, but they certainly were thought to have access to them. Witches could communicate with them, or even travel into their realms, be they hell, fairylands, or somewhere else otherworldly.

Today's Witches work with spirits just as closely, though the language we use varies. Again, we can thank Margaret Murray and those she inspired in the first half of the twentieth century for the idea that

---

6. Marilynne Roach, *The Salem Witch Trials: A Day-by-Day Chronicle of a Community Under Siege* (Lanham, MD: Taylor Trade Publishing, 2004), 307.

Witches actually worshipped a god apart from the Christianity of the day, and that they were part of a different religion altogether as opposed to a heresy of the Church. Now, Witchcraft is a tradition that can potentially exist within innumerable religious frameworks. Some Witches believe that they have patron deities who choose them at various points in their lives for special work, or simply because the gods like them. Others believe we must choose our own deities. If we consider the wide array of world mythologies and the cultures that birthed these gods and goddesses, it's probably safest to say that who does the choosing depends on the deity involved. Different still, some traditions, like initiatory Wicca, have their own unique deities whose names are revealed only upon initiation.

Increasingly, many Witches describe their practice as secular, because they either don't worship or otherwise work with gods, or else their practices exist outside of a single framework. Some reject the word *religion* because of the personal and cultural traumas that have surrounded its use. This may make sense within our own communities to some extent, but it does suggest a somewhat limited understanding of what "religion" may entail. Not all religions revolve around belief in and worship of gods (consider the great variety that exists in East Asian forms of Buddhism, for example). Further, just because people don't identify as religious doesn't mean that others won't recognize what they're doing *as* religious, whether or not that's fair. Evangelical Protestants in the United States, for example, describe themselves as "nondenominational," yet they have clear, distinct practices, values, theologies, and historical origins. Their self-identification serves to send a particular message about belonging and the transcendence of their beliefs beyond a single church; it doesn't actually mean that they don't *behave* as a denomination.

In the same way, secular Witchcraft has largely developed among people who seek to claim an identity outside the popular assumptions about Witchcraft, especially in light of the monopoly that Wicca has held in popular publishing in the last several decades. It's certainly true that not all Witches worship gods, and it's also true that many identify as non-religious entirely. This, however, should not be taken to mean that they don't practice ritual, hold beliefs, and partake in other activities that outsiders would recognize as religious.

All this to say that language may vary wildly, but meanings may carry more similarities than differences. You may not serve a god or have a familiar, but you may speak to trees and stones. Perhaps you're an animist, and you can see and hear the spirits present in the animals, plants, objects, and landscapes around you. You may build special relationships with those spirits, like my Witch friend Acacia, who makes jewelry from stones, bones, and other natural remains. They speak with the objects directly, shaping metal settings or wire-wrapping each piece in accordance with its unique qualities and desires. Their art is one rooted in partnership—the result of a conversation between Witch and spirit. My covenmate Eis has a similar inclination but with plants. She can grow anything (and even regularly reverses the damage I do to my own houseplants). It's not because she's studied horticulture—she's an IT girl all the way. She communicates with the plants themselves because she uniquely understands that they have their own spirits.

Other Witches—especially Traditional Witches—work with land spirits and other spirits of place. This could be relatively simple, like greeting the river near your home as you walk to work, which is what my friend Lukaos does every day. It could also mean leaving regular offerings or physically and financially tending to the ecological well-being of the earth itself. Many practices of Witchcraft depend entirely on location. You bond with the land you live on. If you move, those spirits stay behind where they belong. In some Northern European traditions, these types of spirits are called "wights."[7]

These are only some examples of the spirits that may be a part of a Witch's practice. We can also nuance these further. For example, many atheist Witches could still be said to be working with spirits in that the gods become archetypes—embodiments of particular human qualities. One might erect an altar to Athena not because one believes the Greek goddess is a distinct, superhuman entity with her own agenda, but because one wants to foster wisdom, justice, or victory in one's own life. In a similar fashion, a Witch could hold a ritual to converse with a dead relative because he knows doing so will bring comfort, peace, or closure.

---

7. In other traditions, however, a wight is a spirit of the dead, or even just another word for "spirit" generically. Be sure you understand the context.

He doesn't have to believe the dead can literally hear his words. Spirits and gods may be very real to you, or they may be abstractions. Some magical practitioners even describe creating your own spirits, observing that if you pour enough energy into something, it becomes reality. As a Witch, you take what you have and use it to your advantage. You don't have to hold particular beliefs, other than the belief that you can effect change.

Some Witches even view themselves as the only true gods worth serving. Their magic is designed to bolster and develop themselves. This may sound selfish to some, but consider how important it is to be healthy and centered before we can help others. Consider that we live in a culture that demands that we run ourselves into the ground to serve others—bosses, coworkers, clients, partners, parents, children. Self-care is quite a radical concept still, especially for people in caretaker roles. For some, Witchcraft is a way to return that focus to the self, to recover from trauma, to break destructive social patterns, or to otherwise heal. Sometimes, being selfish is the best thing to be, and these types of Witches will tell you that, as Witches, we *are* sacred beings.

We'll look at devotion and spirit work in another chapter, but now take a moment to ask yourself: Whom does my Witchcraft serve? A god? A community? The land? Myself? Do I have a relationship with any other spirits? What relationships would I like to build?

Witchcraft in the Real World

It's useful to look to history, folklore, and fantasy for inspiration and perspective, but that utility is limited. We're still modern people living in the age that we do, with all its parameters, demands, and expectations. We may fantasize about living perfectly magical lives, but for most of us this will remain a fantasy. We already know that real Witchcraft doesn't look like what we see in movies, but it also doesn't look like the filtered social media posts that we scroll through on a daily basis. More than likely, it doesn't even look like the expectations you set for yourself last week.

How do you develop your Craft in the midst of regular working life? What about when you're dealing with illness? How do you continue to study and learn when all you can think about is your boss, your children, your mortgage, or that unexpected bill? Being a Witch makes you extraordinary, for sure, but it doesn't give you a pass on all the responsibility that comes with living in the real world. Witchcraft is a tool we can use to make some parts of life easier, but in some ways it can also make things a great deal more challenging.

Make no mistake, as exciting and fun as Witchcraft is, it can also be difficult. No matter your path or tradition, you will be required to confront your whole self, and that means the parts that you don't necessarily like. If your path is devotional, the gods and spirits may (and surely will) have their own requirements of you. If you're part of a coven, you'll bear the added weight of a unique sort of social responsibility. Those of you who've been doing this for a while know what I mean when I talk about the challenges of the Craft, especially if your own struggle these days is burnout. Even those of you who are new have likely encountered the experience of being overwhelmed by power and the sheer newness of the experience. It's joyful, but it can also be intimidating, confusing, and frustrating. Whatever your individual practice of the Craft looks like and however far along you may be, if you're growing as a person, accruing power, and encountering others along the way (be they spirits, gods, or other Witches), you will face difficulty. And you'll do it more than once. But you know that! That's why you're reading. Plateaus happen when we get stuck. We may know exactly what the problem is or we may have no clue. The good news is that challenges like these often serve as indicators that we're ready to move forward.

Now that we've talked a bit about what Witchcraft is, we'll start breaking down its fundamental parts. There's magic in going back to our roots, especially if we're old hands. In Zen Buddhism, we find the concept of "beginner's mind," which means that we choose to take on our task without preconceptions. We think and explore as if for the first time. Consider how eager young children are when they first start school or how excited you get when you finally get to try something you've always wanted to do. This is the strategy I'll ask you to take moving forward.

• EXERCISE •
Finding Your Witchcraft

The goal of the following tasks, whichever you choose (and certainly you may choose more than one), is to start peeling away some of your assumptions and expectations about what Witchcraft is and what it can do, even where they've been ingrained over years. Each element takes a slightly different strategy depending on where you are in your own journey, so please revisit the explanations in the introduction as necessary.

Air

If you don't already keep a magical journal, book of shadows, or some other type of reflective notebook or record, now is the time. No excuses. No matter what type of Witchcraft you practice, introspection will serve you well, and one of the most readily available ways to get to know yourself—your goals, your desires, your fears, your hang-ups—is by reflecting on yourself! Your book doesn't have to be fancy. It doesn't even have to be a book! You can type on a computer if you prefer, or even dictate your thoughts into a voice recorder. No one will ever read or listen to your thoughts unless you share them (and I suggest you don't—even where we insist it doesn't, having an audience alters our behavior, so resist the urge to start a blog or social media account for this purpose). No one will check your spelling and grammar or criticize your word choices or your pronunciation. The point of self-reflection is not to turn yourself into a writer, a historian, or an information resource for others; it's just to get your ideas flowing and make a habit of reflection. If writing is overly difficult or physically impossible, that's okay! You can record voice memos on your phone, use a sketchbook to create art, or even collect images into a scrapbook that meaningfully illustrates your thoughts. None of your work has to make sense to anyone else—only you. But choose a method (or explore several at once) and commit to self-reflection over the course of this book.

With all that in mind, contemplate the following questions as thoroughly as you can: Are you a Witch? How do you know? What makes someone a Witch? Where does your understanding of what a Witch is come from? Have you ever met or heard of someone who claimed to be a Witch but who didn't meet this definition? What was their reasoning?

Fire

Witches are extraordinary people because they take control over their lives and work to create change, whether on a large scale or small. Part of being a Witch is developing your personal power, harnessing it, and using it to make magic. As we've discussed, Witchcraft is often scary to outsiders because it challenges the status quo and encourages practitioners to shy away from what is often considered normal. With that in mind, consider your own fears. What do you do or not do because you're afraid of being judged, afraid of failing, or afraid of getting hurt (particularly emotionally—I'm not necessarily asking you to start free climbing!)? Witchcraft helps us to transcend limitations, but only if we take mundane action first. Begin to listen consciously to the voice in your head that tells you not to do things and ask it why. Are your fears reasonable, or are you afraid because the thing at hand is difficult, part of a personal pattern, or rooted in being socially acceptable? Are you afraid to pursue a hobby because you think you're too old or because it's traditionally associated with another gender? Are you afraid to be honest with people because you want their approval? Are you afraid to let go of a toxic relationship because you won't know who you are without it? Are you afraid to pursue a dream because you think it's too hard? Are you afraid to begin something because you're worried you might make a mistake?

Whatever that fear is, take the first step in overcoming it. Begin addressing the little fears that you encounter in your day to day. Which keep you safe, and which hold you back? It's okay to be afraid, but do the thing anyway. Fear is a useful emotion in that it keeps us safe, but if we let it run our lives, it also keeps us from growing. The liberation that comes with facing one's fears and pressing on is beyond any value, and it will be important as you move forward. When in doubt, I like to remember a piece of sage advice from Terry Pratchett, through his character and longstanding favorite literary Witch, Granny Weatherwax: "A witch ought never to be frightened in the darkest forest...because she should know in her soul that the most terrifying thing in the forest was her."[8]

Water

Do you remember what it was that made you first want to be a Witch? For a lot of us, it was the prospect of being able to do magic to improve our lives. For others, it was the glamor that seemed to come with the image of the Witch. Think back on all the things that excited you when you first began studying and practicing. You may even be able to look back in your magical journals and read early entries. What kinds of things occupied your interest? Are you still doing them? Chances are, there are things that you stopped doing because life got in the way. You may not even realize it. There was a point in my own life, for example, when I suddenly realized that I had no idea what phase the moon was in. That I hadn't for a while, in fact. I used to hold rituals in time with the moon, but now I barely paid attention to it at all. I had been a Witch for a long time—I understood intellectually what kind of impact the moon can have on mood, magic, and personal power—but I had nonetheless begun to ignore those basics. I used to be excited about tracking the moon! The simple act of reclaiming that awareness and altering my magical practice to account for lunar tides was a game changer at a low point in my practice.

Consider the early steps in your work as a Witch. Are there things that you used to do that you somehow have lost? Choose one thing and reincorporate it into your practice. Focus on that thing, perhaps for the whole month. Note how it feels. Is it still important to you? If so, how will you build it into your current routine? If not, have you replaced it with something better for you?

Earth

It's a common saying, particularly in eclectic Wiccan spaces, that Witchcraft is whatever you want it to be. Many a writer or speaker will tell you that it's okay to try on a number of beliefs and practices and simply throw out what doesn't fit. There's an element of truth to this. It's true

---

8. Terry Pratchett, *Wintersmith* (New York: HarperCollins Publishers, 2006), 240.

that you are your own authority and that you have the right to decide what's best for yourself. It's also true that no one can tell you what to believe or what's best for your spiritual practice. However, if you only ever choose what feels best, what's most comfortable, and what's most natural to you, you will stunt your progress. This is as true in Witchcraft as it is in learning an instrument or developing as an athlete. You have to tear down muscle to build it stronger, and you have to spend hours running scales and developing hand strength if you want to be a top guitarist. Progress is work. Advancing as a Witch requires that you get uncomfortable.

Sometimes, the things that make us uncomfortable aren't necessarily things that we're scared of, things we've tried before and just didn't like, or things that fundamentally clash with our beliefs. Sometimes—especially for those of us who've been around for a while and are pretty set in our ways—things make us uncomfortable just because we think they're, well, kind of *stupid*.

I came up in the Craft being very suspicious of the New Age and everything I thought went along with it. My Witchcraft—so I thought—was darker, toothier, more serious. I'd roll my eyes when people would go on about balancing chakras, doing yoga, or using crystals in healing. It took a series of encounters with another Witch to change my mind. I'd been the high priestess of a coven for a few years, knew how to work effective magic, and had my routine down, but a slump led me to start exploring new techniques. I ended up taking a class with a teacher in another tradition, figuring I didn't really have anything to lose. This was someone I respected, and had for a while, but suddenly I was being asked to do things I'd always thought of as too New Agey (actually, the word I'd so harshly used previously was *dumb*). But I knew I was only going to get out what I put in, so I rolled with it and decided to trust my teacher.

Wasn't I surprised to find that, whether or not I thought something was silly, sometimes it was still really effective and powerful? I learned a lot, simply by putting aside my personal hang-ups about what was "real" Witchcraft and trying new things. Sure, there are still plenty of pieces of the New Age that don't jibe with my personality or just didn't work out for me. That's okay, and this personal experiment really helped enliven my practice in the end.

Think of those things that fall within or even slightly outside of your personal definition of Witchcraft that you haven't tried seriously (or at all) because they're off-putting. Maybe you think they're stupid, inauthentic, nonsensical, or just silly. Choose one or two things to try, approaching them with beginner's mind. Commit to exploring them for a set period of time (a month is good) so that you know you're being as fair to yourself as possible. Have fun with this! If you still think it's silly at the end, you never have to do it again. But you might surprise yourself.

Chapter 2
Sacred Space

Many introductory books start with instructions for setting up a personal altar. If you've been a Witch for any length of time, you probably already have one, and maybe even more than one for different purposes. If you're a newcomer, you may be in the midst of learning about what each tool is for, where they all go, how to acquire them, and all that fun (sometimes frustrating) stuff. Everyone seems to have a strong opinion about altars, and this makes sense because for a lot of Witches this is where their practice starts. Altars are the abiding favorite for social media posts. We love to decorate them on holidays, and they quickly become focal points for our identities as Witches. Unfortunately, the altar is also where many personal practices *stop*.

It's easy to get lost in materialism and forget that the point of an altar isn't to collect followers on social media or to display expensive tools you don't really need. Personal meaning has a way of seeping away without our realizing it. On the flip side, it's just as easy to forget that the altar—though it is an important sacred space—isn't our *only* sacred space. Too often we forget about our homes, our communities, and even our own bodies! In this chapter, we'll look at what it means for something to be sacred, as well as how and why we create sacred spaces. We'll reconsider personal altars—whether your first or the one you've kept your whole life—and the sacred objects in our lives. Finally, we'll look at how the company we keep and how we take care of ourselves impact our sense of the sacred.

Setting Apart the Sacred

"Wow. It's like Witchcraft threw up in here."

Corvus looked around my living room. I had decided it was finally time to purge. Or at least dust. Twenty-something years of practicing Witchcraft will leave a pretty big mark on your décor, and mine was getting a little out of hand. Aside from the books—which sat haphazardly in piles alongside overflowing shelves—there were tumbled stones, statues, jars full of spell remnants and gods know what else, and mementos from public rituals and festivals I only half remembered. I had moved everything down onto the floor so that I could wipe the shelves, and stuff was strewn everywhere.

"What even is this?" She picked up a faded red cloth sachet tied with a fraying ribbon and gave it a whiff, scrunching her nose. "Whooo...it's expired, whatever it is."

"That's the prosperity charm from that workshop we took at Starwood. Remember?"

"Yeah, that was four years ago."

"Really?" I couldn't remember. It seemed like just last summer. "Are you sure?"

"Yeah. I think it's worked about as well as it's going to." Corvus laughed and raised an eyebrow. "You know, you can't save everything."

Corvus was right, of course. Stuff has a way of accumulating and can take over a space if you let it. For some people, clutter is their aesthetic. It can be charming. When you love something and it takes up a big part of your life, it makes sense that your home would reflect that. My home certainly does! It doubles as a meeting place for my coven, Foxfire, so there are a half-dozen other Witches adding to the chaos.

The thing about unmitigated acquisition, though, is that it tends to stagnate the energy of a place. Have you ever walked into a storage space and the air just felt heavy? Clutter has a way of stopping the flow of a place. To me it feels like the air is too warm and harder to breathe. If I'm in a space like that for too long I may start to feel anxious or irritated without really knowing why. This can be especially true when many of the objects in the space are magical or otherwise carry a lot of heavy emotion with them (think about how powerful photographs or other items belonging to deceased loved ones can be). If you're familiar with the Chinese practice of feng shui, you may have additional insight into this phenomenon. The placement of objects—furniture, décor, and knick-knacks—affects how energy moves in a room.[9] Stuff can lend power to our work and elevate our mood, but it can also stifle us, sometimes without us even realizing it.

That goes both ways too. Maybe the issue isn't clutter or stagnation; maybe it's a simple lack of connection. If you're trying to practice in less than ideal conditions and haven't been able to make the space your own, the end result may be exactly the same. Perhaps you have a less than understanding roommate, or you haven't shared your path with your family and don't want them to inadvertently find out. Maybe you just don't feel like you have the resources to build the space for yourself that you want. Stuff usually costs money, after all. Maybe your magical space isn't serving you because, well, it just doesn't feel very magical to you.

Whatever your particular circumstances are, one thing is clear: your surroundings impact your Witchcraft practice. The sights, smells, sounds, and feel of a place heavily influence us, though we often don't realize exactly how much.

Many Craft teachers advise that one of the most important goals of practice is integration. Your work as a Witch should extend beyond sabbats and full moons. It shouldn't feel totally distinct from your daily life. If you've spent much time in magical communities or have read many books on Witchcraft, you may have already encountered the idea that the distinction between the magical and the mundane is an illusion. Any act may be magical. This is certainly true, and for many Witches this is an admirable goal. However, as with the clutter in your home, there is a line to be walked. Finding magic and connecting with the divine through the everyday is profound where it happens, but it is not always possible, or even desirable. Sometimes life is brutal. Overwhelmingly, Witchcraft

---

9. Interestingly, feng shui was historically very concerned with the burial of the dead and the proper placement of graves to aid spirits to reach the afterlife. In more recent years—thanks at least in part to colonialism and appropriation—feng shui has come to be synonymous with upscale home organization. For more, consider *The Tao of the West: Western Transformations of Taoist Thought* by J. J. Clarke (Routledge, 2000).

traditions are not ascetic. We don't take solace in deprivation or look for spiritual justification in suffering. You don't fail as a Witch when you can't find some cosmic lesson in your soul-sucking job or in the death of a family member, and admonishment that we need to rarely comes from the people in the world who suffer the most. There will be times in your life when your practice as a Witch will be a *refuge* from the everyday.

In the quest to find the spiritual in the mundane, we've forgotten that to be sacred is to be set apart. The word *sacred* itself comes to English from Latin via Old French, and it literally means "to set aside," specifically in reference to objects or places. By definition, the sacred is *not* everywhere and everything.[10] We may find the sacred in surprising places, and it may be subjective and movable, but sometimes insisting that it's everywhere, like clutter, can actually drain and discourage us.

After years of practice, if you're experiencing a lull, consider that your sacred space isn't quite as sacred as it once was. Does sitting before your altar or shrine shift your mood? Does this place where you work your magic still feel special? Are the gods and spirits of your Craft present here? Just because the answer to these questions was "yes" in the past doesn't mean that things haven't changed, perhaps without you even noticing.

New Witches may experience related issues. Our culture is materialistic, and we're inundated by social media with infinite ways to spend money on things we don't need. You may be experiencing a lot of pressure to build an elaborate altar right away or to spend money on fancy tools. But if your sacred space doesn't reflect *you*, it won't have the desired effect in your life. With so many sources telling us how things should be done, where do we start? Just because particular techniques are popular doesn't guarantee that they'll serve you. What do people mean when they say that objects on an altar "speak" to them? Is it okay that your sacred spaces don't look like the posts that circulate on Witch social media sites? How do you ensure that you're building something that will truly aid your developing practice?

---

10. Mircea Eliade, *The Sacred and the Profane: The Nature of Religion* (Orlando, FL: Harcourt, 1957), 11–16.

Cleansing Your Space

Your living environment affects and reflects your well-being. The state of your home often says a lot about your mental state, your priorities, and the amount of control you're currently exercising in your life. It's true for many of us, for example, that when we're busy at work, stressing over school, or otherwise dealing with messy life stuff, dishes don't get done. Laundry lies around unfolded. The bed doesn't get made, or the floor doesn't get vacuumed or swept. This is especially true for many who live with clinical depression, which is an increasing number of us. Your inclination may be to let these things slide because other matters are more pressing, but disorder in your living space could be at the root of your lagging magical practices. Getting your immediate surroundings in order is also a great place to start if this will be your first time creating your own consciously sacred space. Now I'm not saying you need to transform into a clean freak, and what constitutes disorder is certainly a matter of perspective and preference, but if you find yourself walking into your intimate spaces and instantly thinking, "Ugh, I see that, but I'll take care of it later," there's a good chance that the mess is beyond just your aesthetic preference.

When the spaces where your magic lives are in disorder, there's a good chance your magic is too (or will be). Before we cleanse, it's good practice to clean. So put on some music or a favorite movie to play in the background and get to it! It doesn't matter how much space you have. You could live in an environment—like a dorm or a shared bedroom—where your control is limited. But even if you're couch surfing in a friend's living room, take note of what things you *can* control, even if it's only organizing the contents of your bag or suitcase. Whatever chores you've been avoiding, tackle them now. You don't have to do it all at once if you're feeling overwhelmed. Start with the area closest to your altar or working space if you already have one, and move outward as you can. Get things off the floor, throw away any bits of stray garbage (if you're anything like me, that means piles of junk mail and papers that just haven't made their way to the recycle bin), and dust. Remember, this is laying the groundwork for Witchcraft, so if it helps motivate you, think of this as itself a magical or devotional act. Go back to some of those magical cleaning techniques you've likely encountered in other books and just haven't tried in a while: as you sweep or vacuum, imagine that you're also clearing out negativity, stagnant energy, or other ethereal grime, along with the dirt. If visualization and imagination are difficult, use your voice to declare the space cleansed and purified. Uttering words with conviction and authority is just as effective as seeing something in your mind's eye. Sweep away from you, toward the door, and outside. Sprinkle salt water afterward to further cleanse and purify the area. I also like to carry a censer around the space, usually burning some blend of frankincense, myrrh, sandalwood, and lavender (all of which have long been associated in various traditions with purification).

When you're done, it's time to move on to your own body! Take a shower or bath. Get as ritualized about it as you want. Cleaning can be a hard, dirty job, and on a practical level you're just washing the mess off. On an energetic level, you're renewing yourself and preparing for a greater act of magic. Some Witches will use consecrated oils and strew herbs in their bathwater (be sure to wrap them in cheesecloth or something similar so they don't clog your drain). I prefer plain salt and a cup of tea on the ledge. Do whatever makes you feel refreshed. When you're done, you can choose to be skyclad or to work in a fresh set of clothes or a ritual robe.

If you've been working as a Witch for a long time, the next part may be especially challenging. You're going to strip your ritual space! Your altar, your shrine, or whatever other place you've built to practice your Craft— you're going to clear it off. This can be a very unsettling thing to undertake, but trust me here. You may want to have a cardboard box, a dust cloth, and whatever cleaning and storage supplies you feel may be necessary. If this will be your first altar, you won't have anything to clear, which is great! This will be an opportunity to start off with a strong foundation. Focus on clearing a space for yourself: a dresser top, an end table, a windowsill, or some other surface you can dedicate to magical work. You can then read the next few paragraphs for perspective if you like, or just skip to the part where we begin building.

Before you begin, take a moment to reflect on the objects in front of you. Which have you had the longest? Which was the most expensive?

The hardest to acquire? Which did you make yourself? Place your hands on some surface of this space and try to feel the energy of it. Does it still flow the way it should? Does being here still signal to your brain that magic is afoot and the gods and spirits are present? If you've felt your practice stagnating, there's a good chance that some of the problem lies right here. It sounds obvious enough that we need to tend to our sacred spaces in order to help maintain our spiritual health, but it's surprisingly easy to allow things to fall into disorder and neglect. Dust has a way of becoming invisible as soon as it settles. Offerings have a way of sitting out a day or two longer than intended. If you're like most people, you're not immune to such lapses, no matter your intentions.

Contemplate each object in your magical space. One at a time, clean them and remove them, tucking them safely into a box or otherwise storing them out of sight. Do this slowly, but in one sitting. Let the significance of each object sit with you for a moment. Note when and where you find significance lacking or absent altogether. Do this for everything, including candles, dishes, and any altar cloth you may use. When you're done, your space should be completely bare.

When I first did this, I was enormously uncomfortable. I've maintained an altar in my bedroom for twenty-something years, wherever I've lived. Some of my most precious ritual items have been with me that entire time. My chalice is a ceramic cup purchased at an art festival when I was sixteen. My candleholders were found at a thrift store when I was much younger than even that. The antlers were a present from my uncle, a hunter. The clay pentacle and goddess statues are both the products of an art class I took as a senior in high school. The various magical knick-knacks are from my travels, my friends, and the encounters I've had with both the gods and other practitioners over the years. But I also discovered things that no longer served, and even things that now had painful associations. Things that I didn't notice in my day-to-day but were nonetheless occupying my space, impacting it without my awareness. My altar, though I had been tending it and working at it for decades, still held surprises for me. It was bizarre and disquieting to be confronted by an empty space.

If you're uncomfortable, allow yourself to be so. This is a contemplative exercise, so allow yourself to experience it fully, whatever you feel. When you're ready, perform whatever further magical cleansing your tradition—or your intuition—may require. My go-to is a simple consecration with salt water and incense. You may prefer an herbal wash, anointing with oil, or the use of affirmations to declare the space clear and ready for rededication. You may choose to let it sit empty for a designated period of time, perhaps in accordance with the moon (consider disassembling on the new moon and rebuilding on the full) or until a day sacred to whatever gods or spirits you may work with (or just one that's special to you personally). You may also begin reconstruction immediately, if you feel ready.

Take this process more slowly than you did disassembly, perhaps over the course of many days. Begin with your altar cloth, if you use one. Then, add one item at a time, beginning with the most foundational or the most important. Continue your contemplation as you add to your altar. What is the significance of this object? What does it add to your practice?

You stripped your altar in one sitting, but you likely won't reassemble it in one. Allow each object to settle, getting a sense of how it feels working with the whole. Perhaps add one thing per day. Take as much time as required to build and reaffirm your connection with the magical space and all the items in it. When finished, perform whatever dedication your personal practice or your intuition may require. Your space, freshly cleaned and reexamined, will be reenergized. It will have a stronger flow to it and feel more inviting.

First time sacred space creators probably won't have tons of stuff to put on an altar, and that's okay. Various traditions of Witchcraft call for different kinds of tools and arrangements, anyway, and perhaps you're not even at the point where you're thinking about practicing any specific style of Witchcraft at all. You're better off starting with very few things—each of which being heavily meaningful—than with lots of stuff acquired just because someone else told you that you should have it. Instead, try this: leave the surface that you chose for yourself empty except for a single candle (and whatever holder it requires to burn safely). Color, shape, and materials don't matter at this point. Just choose one that feels special to you. Every time you're in your sacred space, light the candle. If you want to pray, meditate, or perform some other kind of spiritual exercise while it burns, you may. But also light it when you're studying from magical books, when you're journaling, when you're conversing with other Witches online, or when you're simply sitting in contemplation. The point is to draw your attention to your new spiritual focus and to train yourself to be mindful when you're in this space. You get to decide exactly what that looks like. If you can't burn a candle, go outside and collect a palm-size stone. Use it to remind yourself of the foundations you're building. Hold it in contemplation, keep it close when you're doing any kind of magical work, and reflect on what it means to be connected to the world every time you look at it.

From this simple beginning, you may add other tools over time, as informed by whatever tradition you might feel called to, or whatever your intuition suggests. You might choose to add natural objects—like acorns or shells—which reflect your region. You might add photos of dead loved ones, images of deities that inspire you, any divination tool you might acquire, your magical journal, or any other objects that otherwise inspire you. I like to decorate my altar space with my own artwork, which is of a magical nature. I also keep tokens that symbolize my relationships with loved ones, projects and goals I have, and sometimes even the books I'm currently studying. The point is that your altar isn't about spending money or acquiring lots of things that aren't immediately meaningful to you. Eventually, you may choose to seek out traditional tools, like a cauldron, a wand, or a ritual knife of some kind, but allow those things to come into your life as needed. You don't *need* any of them to be a Witch. What you do need is a sense of connection and an understanding that you can use potentially *anything* to work magic.

Consecrating and (Re)connecting with Your Tools

We don't *need* anything, it's true, but that doesn't seem to stop us from acquiring things! Whatever our traditions or personal paths, Witches love stuff. Perhaps it's because we train ourselves to work with the magic present in all things and because we naturally see potential where others may see only plain old *stuff*. Many of us are born collectors, barely able to venture out without bringing home interesting bits from the natural landscape (I have a weakness for interesting rocks) or old trinkets discarded by other people, along with jars, pouches, cords, and other scraps with the makings of spell ingredients. My own home lies somewhere on the border between natural history museum and gingerbread cottage. Any other Witch would recognize it as a magical household just because, energy aside, we tend to have similar patterns.

Our different traditions call for different tools, however. As a Gardnerian Wiccan, my ritual practice is often a little more ceremonial than many other kinds of Witches'. We have a lot of specialized tools: the athame, the wand, the altar pentacle, the chalice, and many others besides. Other Witches may use stangs, cords, cauldrons, scourges, prayer beads, divination tools like tarot cards and runes, crystals, and countless other things. It's likely too that over the years you've accumulated more than you actually need or use. It's very common for newcomers to Witchcraft to feel like they need to run out and acquire a lot of tools quickly. Then, once they've actually had the opportunity to use them, they figure out that actually they're much more drawn to something else (or don't feel the need for the thing at all!). That wasn't quite the right athame, or you actually prefer working with a wand and not a blade at all. Practically every book and teacher out there tell us to take our time, but sometimes we just can't help rushing in.

Once we have our new precious objects, we will usually consecrate them somehow. This may be simple or very complex. A crystal may only be left under moonlight or bathed in salt water, while a ritual sword may be carved or etched with particular magical symbols.

I've noticed something, though. For a lot of us, we consecrate a tool when it's new, and then we don't give any thought to its maintenance. Think about the tools you've had the longest. When was the last time you cleansed and reconsecrated them? Objects, even inherently magical objects that require very little attention (like crystals), pick up the energy of the space they're living in and of the people who handle them. Simply being regularly used in ritual isn't assurance that a tool is always fit for that purpose. When was the last time you cleansed your athame or chalice? Or whatever other tools you may have been relying on for years? One of the things that surprised me when I was taking apart and reconstructing my altar was how long it had been since I had blessed and cleansed my own tools. No wonder they weren't quite up to par! No wonder things weren't feeling quite as magical as I wanted.

I got my first athame when I was sixteen. It's a cheap, mass-produced, nondescript little blade that came in a cardboard box stamped with "made in Pakistan." I say cheap because experience and a steady income have altered my perspectives since then, but truth be told it was quite a precious thing for a teen Witch with few magical resources, relying on the minimum wage earned at summer jobs. Never mind having to persuade my parents! Since I was under eighteen, I couldn't just go out and buy any sort of weapon on my own, even a dull knife that wouldn't be cutting anything. It took a lot of planning and a lot of work to buy that first athame! Consequently, I cherished it. I wrote my own consecration ritual, which entailed a lot of anointing with oil (plain old olive oil from the grocery store, because I was still just a newbie and didn't have the knowledge or resources for essential oils or fancy carriers…it works just as well, by the way), salt water, and incense smoke. I also carved the handle to include my Craft name and a series of magical symbols that held significance for me. I turned the handle black by burning it in a candle flame and then rubbing it down with wax. When it wasn't resting on my bedroom altar, I kept it wrapped in a scrap of black fabric.

Since those early years, I've acquired other ritual blades. A regular paycheck and my own space have allowed me to own more costly—even customized—athames and swords. But, you know, not one of those has ever been more magical than that first athame. Not because of anything but the energy and time I put into it. Almost twenty years since I bought it, it's still my athame, and I've chosen it again and again over many more expensive blades. It doesn't matter how much you spend or how unique the tool is; it's about how you value it.

Not every tool you run across over the course of your life will have that level of impact. Some of your magical objects will come and go as your practice develops. You'll try things that won't speak to you in the long run or that only serve you at particular points in your life. Some of your tools may very well be better off packed up in that box you prepared when you cleared your altar.

As you build or rebuild your ritual space, pay special care to each of your tools. New Witches, acquire your first tools as slowly as you need to, focusing on one at a time and learning to use each on its own, before its surrounded by others. Experienced Witches, you don't have to try to go back in time and recapture those first feelings of connection—I'm not the same Witch I was when I was sixteen, and you've no doubt changed as you've grown too—but you can revisit that same level of care that first went into them. Take your time and consecrate your tools. Cleanse them. Reconnect to them, or connect for the first time. Commit them to their purpose of serving you. At the end of this chapter, you'll find a variety of exercises for this purpose.

You Are What You Hang With

Sacred space isn't only made up of our homes, temples, altars, and tools. It's also our physical and energetic bodies, which are heavily impacted by the people we spend time with. We'll discuss self-care shortly, but first I want us to take a close look at how our social environments can impact us magically, which in turn comes home to roost in our sacred space.

Remember in school when you hit adolescence and your class sort of naturally divided into cliques and social groups? Athletes hung out with athletes; nerds, punks, honor students, and theater kids all found their tribes between classes; and it could be traumatic to find that you didn't fit comfortably in any of them. Popular movies like *Mean Girls* and *The Craft* make a point of showing how the formation of cliques impacts young people, especially when that impact is negative. Whether or not these groups really exist in every high school or if they're just stereotypes exaggerated for our entertainment, we recognize that people tend to congregate in groups with others who look and act like themselves. Further, we make assumptions about others based on what groups they belong to. In *The Craft*, that Witchy favorite from the nineties, new student Sarah initially spurns the advances of school heartthrob Chris after his friends make fun of her in class. He assures her that "those guys are assholes" and that he isn't like them. She retorts, "You are what you hang with." In short, hanging with assholes makes you an asshole.

I'm not suggesting that we use *The Craft* as a basis for our social values, but Sarah has a point: who you spend your time with has an impact on your character. More importantly for our purposes, it impacts how you relate to the sacred as well as what sorts of energies you carry into your sacred space!

Even more than ritual tools or other kinds of inanimate objects, people generate energy that has very real consequences for others in their immediate space. Have you ever walked into a room full of people and instantly known that something terrible had just happened? Or felt kind of down in the dumps but then gone to a party with friends and cheered up? Have you ever noticed how depressed and unhappy people tend to hang out with others who have similar struggles? Or how bubbly, joyful people tend to attract others like themselves? Wherever we go, we tend to congregate with like minds, whether that means people with similar backgrounds and interests or people with similar attitudes and experiences.

In some contemporary versions of the Hermetic tradition, which lies at the root of many Western occult systems, including Wicca and some other traditions of Witchcraft, we find the principle of vibration, which states that everything, at its most basic level, is in motion. Objects, living things, our thoughts, and even abstract concepts like love, hatred, and divinity have frequencies—rates of vibration.[11] Things tend to vibrate at the rate of whatever is around them, and as magicians, we can control our own mental vibration. This is what people mean when they talk about their "vibes." Many people believe that how we vibrate impacts what we attract into our lives. It can sound a little flaky on social media sites when paired with pictures of crystals and waif-like models selling life-coaching services, but this is actually a foundational principle in

---

11. Three Initiates, *The Kybalion: Centenary Edition* (New York: TarcherPerigee, 2018), 17–18. This is not a Hermetic text per se, nor are its principles historical, but its influence on modern magic is nonetheless undeniable. In the United States, especially, much of what is popularly understood about Hermeticism is heavily impacted by New Thought, a nineteenth-century American religious movement. Though it is beyond the scope of this book, even a cursory exploration of New Thought reveals startling insight into the evolution of several contemporary traditions of Witchcraft.

many systems of magic. In many New Age communities, courtesy of the influence of New Thought, practitioners know this principle as the "Law of Attraction," which states that you attract the energy that you send out into the world. Sometimes you'll hear the saying "like attracts like." These are related ideas. You may have also encountered this principle through the practice of sympathetic magic, wherein you work your will on a person or situation by incorporating materials and symbols that are related to and reflective of the object of the spell. You want to heal a loved one of an illness, so you take their image (maybe a photo or a poppet in their likeness) and surround it with healing herbs or green candles (for health), all while envisioning them healthy. You want to attract healing, so you send out healing energy. You want to bring love into your life, so you send out love. Whatever your desire or intention, you surround yourself with things that correspond with that desire or intention. This is one of the most basic principles of magic.

In recent years, the Law of Attraction has come under deserved scrutiny in magical communities, as people use it to justify suffering, poverty, and oppression, however unintentionally. If we can create our own realities with our thoughts, then are people responsible for the bad things that happen to them? Most Witches—I hope—would say of course not. Our attitudes, our choices, and our circumstances are determined by myriad factors, many of which are objectively beyond our individual control. As Witches, however, we take what control we can, and there's a lot of merit to the idea that like attracts like.

Just like in those teen movies, mean people really do tend to be friends with other mean people (and Sarah's first impression was right: Chris was indeed an asshole). Dysfunctional people tend to congregate with dysfunctional people. Whether by circumstance or by choice, human beings tend to form groups made up of others who share their values, their interests, and their beliefs.

Who you hang out with affects your practice of Witchcraft. Your personhood is impacted by your social circle, and both are components of the sacred in your life. Just like the décor of your ritual space and the magical tools on your altar, the people in your life can help or hinder you. Part of building your sacred spaces involves considering who you share them with. We tend to take on the characteristics of the people around us. It's great to be exposed to difference and to be challenged beyond our comfortable social bubbles. I'm certainly not suggesting that you only hang out with people like yourself. That's not how growth happens! But sometimes we take on the energy of the people in our lives, often without realizing it. We pick up their habits and participate in their struggles. We become players in their dramas. We can't help it! And we bring all of that home with us, even if we aren't aware of it. So make sure you're being judicious about with whom you spend your time. Make sure you aren't allowing others to get in the way of your own Craft development. When you want to become a better athlete or a better musician, you train and play with athletes and musicians who are more experienced than you and who will challenge you to push forward. It's no different in magic. When you want to grow in your practice of Witchcraft, hang out with Witches who inspire you! Make new contacts online or in person. Check out new authors and teachers. Visit new events. Look for people who are doing what it is you want to be doing. Surround yourself with people who encourage you to be better. It's much easier to cultivate curiosity, passion, and thoughtfulness when you're hanging out with people who are curious, passionate, and thoughtful.

In situations where you must be with people who drain or discourage you, learn to shield yourself. Be conscious that others can have very real impact on your emotional and magical state and take precautions where necessary.

Shielding

Shielding is the magical process by which we energetically protect ourselves from outside forces. That could mean the negativity radiating off your boss after a long day at work, the stress that comes from scrolling through your social media feed and absorbing the collective anxiety, or, in rare cases, the workings of other Witches and magicians who don't have your best interests at heart. Your body and your psyche are at the center of your sacred space, and they require their own kind of maintenance. As an introverted person who sometimes gets overwhelmed by lots of human contact—and for years I worked at a high school, so this was an especially critical issue for me—I shield myself all the time to keep other peoples' energy from leaving me wiped out at the end of the day. I've also used shielding to escape someone's notice (this is a great trick for dodging exes in public places or encouraging the teacher to call on someone else in class).

Being able to protect yourself from outside energies is a valuable skill for any Witch, whether you're worried about the usual gunk that we tend to accumulate just moving around in the world, or you're undertaking intense ritual with entities that warrant an extra layer of padding on your psyche. Unfortunately, shielding is one of those things that is so foundational to magical practice that it frequently gets overlooked by beginners and neglected by advanced Witches. But just like how we tend to get sick when we fail to eat healthy foods and drink enough water, forgetting to shield can leave us energetically vulnerable, both in ritual space and out. Luckily, there are lots of simple ways to shield. Here's a quick one that I use all the time:

1. If you have the time and space to do so, put yourself into a meditative state by whatever means you prefer. If you're totally new to the Craft, sit quietly and focus on your breathing. Feel your connection to the ground beneath you. Allow yourself to be aware of your body and to be as present as possible.

2. Imagine a barrier forming between yourself and your surroundings. What type of barrier you envision can change depending on what you're trying to keep out. Because my name is Thorn, I like to imagine a tangle of thorny vines growing around me (remember the Disney version of *Sleeping Beauty*?). My Witch friend Corvus likes to imagine a brick wall. You may imagine yourself encased in a sphere of protective light, behind a wall of actual shields, or being guarded by familiar spirits or other entities. If this kind of visualization is a barrier for you, it's just as effective to use other strategies. You could physically trace a circle around yourself and then declare that you are protected, even when you step out of it. You could also recite an incantation or affirmation to signal to yourself that your shields are

up, even something simple like: "I activate my shield. No harmful energies or intentions can touch me."

3. Focus on this image and strengthen it with your will. Declare yourself protected from outside forces that would harm you. With every exhale, imagine the strength of your shield growing.

Use your shield on a daily basis to maintain your energetic health but especially when in uncomfortable company or circumstances. We can't always control who we spend our time with or where, but we can magically keep ourselves from allowing other people's energetic crap to glom onto us.

Self-Care

Tending to your sacred space also means tending to yourself! Your body, your mental state, and your emotional health all have bearing on your spiritual development and your progress as a Witch. Constructing a beautiful and nurturing space for your Craft practice is wonderful, but it only goes so far if you're not also taking care of yourself.

There are some Witches who take this to mean that they should adopt a particular diet or exercise routine. For some, this may be helpful. When I was in my early twenties and becoming more serious about my practice of Wicca, I decided that doing no harm (which is how I interpreted the Wiccan Rede at the time) meant that I should strive for a vegan lifestyle. I began eliminating animal products of all kinds from my life, and this was an important part of my spiritual practice. I made other choices as I got older (in fact, now I'm a licensed hunter), and these are no less valid. To live a healthier, more fulfilling life, you may decide to alter your eating habits, your workout routine (if you even have one), your buying habits, or any number of other things.

The key is this: everyone's self-care will look different. What's right for your body and your emotional well-being may be totally wrong for someone else. To give you another example, consider how we treat mental health issues. I take medication to manage depression and anxiety, which I've had for most of my life. I also see specialized doctors and psychotherapists as necessary, but those medications are critical for my well-being. For whatever reason, my brain just doesn't produce all the mood-regulating chemicals that neurotypical brains do. My medications could actually be harmful to a neurotypical person, but I need them! Others may require other kinds of medicines or special care. I have friends who take insulin, testosterone, estrogen, and more medications than I could list here. Some bodies need chemical assistance to function well. Some bodies require wheelchairs or walkers or braces. Some bodies benefit from massage, chiropractic adjustment, or acupuncture. Some bodies have allergies and need to stick to strict diets. Some thrive on vegetarian or raw diets. Others need animal protein. Some bodies are fat, while others are skinny. Some are athletic and muscular.

Your body is unique to you, and no one else can tell you exactly what your self-care should look like. What's important for your Witchcraft practice is that you are *mindful* about that self-care. Have you neglected your body along with your sacred space? They are linked.

Self-care might mean adopting an exercise routine or making a change in your diet, but it could just as easily mean getting enough sleep at night or treating yourself to a manicure because it relaxes you and makes you feel beautiful. If you're an introvert, it might mean learning to take time away and set better social boundaries. If you struggle with spending, it might mean learning to budget or cutting up your credit card. Self-care for many, especially further in their practice of Witchcraft, often entails some kind of therapy or counseling. Only you can decide what is right for your own routine, but be mindful as you explore that "self-care" has become a buzzword and now represents a growing consumer market. It's become common for businesses to advertise their products as essential and justifiable on these grounds. Be aware of where someone seeking a profit may be trying to manipulate you ("Indulge yourself! You deserve it!"). Self-care does not inherently cost money, and probably shouldn't most of the time.

Self-care includes all aspects of your being: body, mind, relationships, and finances, as well as spirituality. Small changes can have a huge impact where your Craft practice is concerned. Sometimes, the key to advancing your Witchcraft is making sure you're properly tending to your mundane life.

Whether you're an overwhelmed beginner worried about how to get started or an old hand who just feels the walls of your practice closing in around you, it's worthwhile to start by looking at your physical surroundings. That means your altar, your home, your body, your mind, and your social environment. Small changes often make a big difference. These tiny acts can also motivate you to take additional steps forward by getting your personal magical power flowing. Just like adopting a new exercise routine or a new diet, it's better to pace yourself and make small changes bit by bit rather than over-committing and failing on day three of a new routine that was too ambitious to start. Whatever your long-term goals as a Witch are, your environment should support and encourage you. Change your space, change your life!

• EXERCISE •
Building Sacred Space

The purpose of the following exercises is to create sacred space. Some of these techniques are more elaborate, pulling from other occult traditions or requiring that you get outside and, perhaps, a bit out of your comfort zone. Choose whichever appeals to you most, or try them all.

Air

Many Witches use things like cedar or mugwort bundles to cleanse space in preparation for magical work or just to clear away negativity. You may have also noticed how simply lighting a candle—even one that is unconsecrated and otherwise non-magical—can instantly transform the feeling in a room. What many new Witches do not realize, however, is that all the elements, and not just Air and Fire, are useful for clearing, cleansing, and building sacred space. The elements are not their physical representations, but rather energies that encompass ways of being. They are each capable of clearing space. What's more, combining all four—Earth, Air, Fire, and Water—is even more effective.

You will need physical representations of each element: a dish of salt or soil to represent Earth, a flame to represent Fire, incense or a fan to represent Air, and a dish of water to represent Water. Place these on your altar or on some other surface in the space you wish to make sacred. Begin with whichever element feels most appropriate to you. Many start with Air because it is associated in Western occult traditions with the east, the dawn, and therefore beginnings. Others choose to start with Earth because it is associated with foundations and the moment of silence that occurs before creation begins. Your personal associations can inform your choices here—there isn't a singular correct way.

Stand at the center of the space. One at a time, you will carry these representations around in a circular fashion (if you're working in a magic circle, you may do this as part of its construction). Sprinkle the salt or soil lightly around the space, and as you do, say:

> *I cleanse this space with [salt/soil]*
> *and dedicate it by the powers of Earth.*

Do the same with the incense (you may use any kind) or simply waft the fan as you move (for years, I used a large turkey feather acquired from a hunter friend). As you move around the space, say:

> *I cleanse this space with [incense/my fan]*
> *and dedicate it by the powers of Air.*

For Fire, carry your lit candle or lamp around your space and say:

> *I cleanse this space with light*
> *and dedicate it by the powers of Fire.*

Finally, carry your bowl of water around, sprinkling it on the ground as you move and say:

> *I cleanse this space with water*
> *and dedicate it by the powers of Water.*

When you're done, move back to the center of your space and say:

> *By my power and the power of the elements,*
> *I cleanse and consecrate this space.*

It is done. You may move on to other magical work, or simply enjoy your freshly sanctified environment.

This small ritual is heavily inspired by Wiccan Witchcraft, but you are welcome to modify it in accordance with your own frameworks. It's also good to know that any one elemental power can cleanse and purify an object—you don't necessarily need four.

Fire

Clearing and blessing a space can be a drawn-out, elaborate process, but sometimes there just isn't time for all that. To cleanse and consecrate space quickly, try keeping a spray bottle full of consecrated water on hand in your ritual area. You can then simply spray your space before a working, or whenever things are starting to feel a little stagnant. You can even use it on yourself in the place of clearing with smoke (if you are non-Native and have been using sage smudge sticks and are concerned about the appropriation of Indigenous practices, this is an excellent alternative).

You're going to start by infusing a clear alcohol (like vodka, Everclear, or rubbing alcohol) with herbs associated with purification. You may choose frankincense or myrrh resin, rosemary, anise, mugwort, garden sage, cedar, apple, or numerous others. You can use either fresh or dried herbs. Place the herbs into a clean glass jar with a screw lid, and then cover them with the alcohol, allowing the liquid to sit above the herbs. Allow the herbs to soak for several days in a dark place (up to about two weeks), shaking the jar every day. If you wish to make this process even more effective, begin on a new moon, and allow them to infuse until the full moon. Strain the herbs out of the alcohol using a piece of cheesecloth, collecting it in a bowl or another bottle. Then dilute your infusion with water. If you choose, you may use water collected during a rainstorm, water blessed under the moon, or any other sort of ritually collected water relevant to your personal practice. Use a ratio of about four parts water to one part alcohol infusion. If you like, mix in an essential oil associated with purification: lavender, myrrh, rosemary, frankincense, peppermint, or others. Then bottle your completed potion in a clean spray bottle! If you work with crystals, you may even choose to put a small piece of clear quartz directly in the spray bottle to augment its effectiveness.

Before you use it, bless the mixture according to your tradition or intuition. You may dedicate it to your patron deities or spirits you work with, if you have them. You may also simply place both hands on the bottle and recite the following, modifying it or otherwise adding your own embellish-ments as you prefer:

I bless and consecrate this water
by my own powers and by the power of the moon.
I charge it so that it may cleanse and empower all that it touches.
So mote it be.

Use your now-enchanted spray bottle at will, especially when you need to cleanse and purify a ritual space but are short on time or energy.

Water

You could be a Witch for years and years and never touch any kind of ceremonial magic, but sometimes in order to get out of a rut it's worth picking up new tricks from other magical systems. The Lesser Banishing Ritual of the Pentagram (LBRP) is a foundational ritual in many magi-cal traditions but especially those directly linked to the Hermetic Order of the Golden Dawn. You don't have to have a specific religious or mag-ical affiliation to practice it, but it works best if you understand what's behind it, as its structure is very clearly rooted in occult interpretations of esoteric Judaism and Christianity. Since the Golden Dawn disbanded and its ideas circulated more freely, a number of variations exist, and the ritual has been modified to suit different religious paradigms.[12] I've seen contemporary Pagans remove the names of YHVH (the God of ancient Israel) entirely and replace them with the sacred names of their own pan-theons. I've seen some occult orders include Asherah, the female princi-ple of God in some traditions. Others remain true to older versions of the text. I recommend researching these variations and choosing one to

---

12. The appropriation of Jewish traditions by occultists is an important conversation, and across communities a lot of debate exists about the appropriateness of practices like the LBRP. I present it here because of its ubiquity and utility, but if this style of magic appeals to you, you should work to familiarize yourself with its historical contexts. Qabalah has heavily impacted much of Western European occultism, and by extension Witchcraft, even if it is less overt than in this particular instance. It is important to make informed choices to ensure that our contemporary practices do not contribute to the marginalization of other people.

perform consistently for a month or two before making any significant modifications, just so the changes you do choose to make are grounded in experience and not the result of preconceptions or assumptions about other religious traditions.

What's important here is function, and the LBRP has several (that make more or less sense depending on your particular worldview, religious paradigm, and the version you've chosen to use):

First, there is the simple act of cleansing a space. It's not uncommon to find magicians who perform the ritual before erecting the temple in a new place, especially when in public (for example, in a hotel suite or conference room before teaching a magical workshop or performing a public function). I find that it very quickly and very thoroughly neutralizes a space, and I've used it this way myself.

Second, many use it to center and align themselves. This, I find, is much more valuable than the above. Part of what we're doing here is throwing off the astral garbage we've collected by just being alive and moving through the world, and then calling on divine protection. If you incorporate chakra systems and auras into your practice, you can think of it as aligning your chakras or cleansing your personal energy. If language like that puts you off, think of it as centering yourself in preparation for other work. Like magically warming up before tackling something bigger. For me, it's a trigger: "Okay, Mooney, get it together. You're a divine-child-of-the-universe and made-of-stardust and whatever. Time to act like it."

Finally—and most importantly—the LBRP opens a channel between you and things-that-are-bigger-than-you. In Hermetic Qabalah (which is at the root of Western esoteric tradition, and by extension Wicca, though most Wiccans don't use this kind of language), the Tree of Life diagrams the creation of the universe as well as the path to the divine. It's not a timeline, but rather a constant flow of energy, beginning with the first, inaudible breath before the Word of God to the physical earth and our puny, rotting bodies. What's glorious is that, though we are puny and rotting, we're still a part of that perfect system, still imbued with that divine breath. Because of that, we can travel on the Tree. Each sephirah (each sphere on the Tree) is a moment in creation, with its own correspondences and lessons, and the paths drawn between them each hold a lifetime's worth of spiritual work. The LBRP doesn't just banish negative woo and spiritual gunk; it "banishes" the bondage of Malkuth (Kingdom, Earth) and allows us to transcend to heavenly realms.

This means that it creates a channel through which we can more clearly hear the voice of God (or the gods, if you prefer), connect with our higher natures, and see things that are bigger than our immediate problems. When you need to get outside your own head, when you're seeking divine insight, and when you just need to feel like you're not alone in the wilderness, this is a great place to start.

Many magical teachers advise performing this ritual twice a day, or even three times a day. I personally go through phases—especially when I need to refocus and get myself together—where I'll work the LBRP regularly. It comes and goes, and every time I think, "Man, this is fantastic. Why don't I do this more?"

The Lesser Banishing Ritual of the Pentagram is actually a series of rites, practiced in succession. This is the version I learned first, modified from publicly available Golden Dawn materials:

1. Begin in the east, the direction associated in the Hermetic tradition with beginnings, the dawn, and the element of Air.

2. First, perform the rite of the Qabalistic Cross. This includes the intonation of a prayer, "Atoh, Malkuth, Ve-Gedulah, Ve-Geburah, Le-Olahm," while crossing your body in the shape of the Tree. Don't stress about pronunciation at this stage if the language is unfamiliar—it will develop as you learn and practice. Begin at the brow, and with each word move to the next point: pointing to the feet, touching the left shoulder, touching the right shoulder, and then bringing the palms together at the chest.

3. Now it's time to create the circle. Still standing in the east, draw a banishing Earth pentagram (with your hand, your sword, or your athame), which starts in the bottom left and moves up. Intone the first name of God (in this version, we're beginning

with AShRH, Ah-sher-ah, the feminine principle of God). You can visualize the pentagram glowing before you or light pouring out of your lungs as you sound it out. As you do, make what's called the "sign of the Enterer," which entails stepping forward with your right foot and extending your hands through the pentagram, like you're diving. Intoning the name and performing this motion should exhaust you. Pour yourself into it. Be loud, if it helps (there's a way to do this silently too). When you've stretched your arms forward and finished singing the name, return by stepping back into the "sign of silence," which is actually just stepping your feet back together and bringing your left finger to your lips like you're shushing someone in a library.

Move to the south, west, and north. The actions are the same, but the names are different. In the south, intone the name ADNI (A-don-ai, "Lord"). In the west, AHIH (Eh-ei-eh, "I am"). In the north, AGLA (Ah-gay-lah; this is an abbreviation of Atheh Gibor Leolahm Adonai, "to thee be the power until the ages, O Lord").

4. Facing east, perform what is called "the Grand Conjuration." Stand in the middle of your space, gesturing to the directions (with a hand or with your sword) as you call them: "Before me Raphael; behind me Gabriel; on my right hand Michael; on my left hand Uriel." Then say, "For about me flame the pentagrams, and in the middle pillar shines the six-rayed star."

5. End by performing the Qabalistic Cross one last time.[13]

Earth

Tools have a way of becoming invisible to us. When we use them for years, over and over, they sometimes lose the power to trigger the mental shift that working magic requires. This is especially true if you've been practicing

---

13. For another version of the Lesser Banishing Ritual of the Pentagram as well as more detailed explanation, consult Israel Regardie, *The Golden Dawn: The Original Account of the Teachings, Rites, and Ceremonies of the Hermetic Order*, ed. John Michael Greer (Woodbury, MN: Llewellyn Publications, 2018), 360–67.

for a long time, and especially if you're dealing with the weight of leading a coven, training students, or organizing events for a community. This is doubly true if other people routinely handle your tools. Remember when you were a new Witch and every freshly acquired tool and newly learned invocation was enough to push you into a magical mindset all by itself? Just the excitement of trying something new could energize you. When you get tired or stressed out and your magical work stagnates, it can be worthwhile to recapture the energy that accompanies novelty.

We can't go back in time, but we *can* play with novelty and newness while simultaneously challenging ourselves to learn new things. With that in mind, your task is to build your altar or otherwise construct your magical space using entirely different tools. That doesn't mean you have to rush out and buy or make new tools (in fact, I recommend that you challenge yourself not to buy a thing). It just means to try mixing things up a bit.

When I did this, I got way out of my comfort zone and built a traditional-style Wiccan altar—with elemental representations, goddess and god iconography, and a blade for directing power—entirely using crystals and stones that I already had in my possession. I had never felt drawn to using crystals or minerals in magic and I wanted to give it a shot, while at the same time shaking up my lagging personal practice. This kind of set-up might have been very easy and intuitive for another Witch, but for me it was difficult because I tend to be very into high ceremony and traditional, human-made tools. I'd come to rely on my steel athame, my ceramic censer, and my wood and resin statuary. Furthermore, crystals had always made me feel a little silly, thanks to my own prejudices and hang-ups about the New Age.

College students, prisoners, and Witches living in certain kinds of more regulated housing situations face similar challenges, so this is a worthwhile skill to have. How will you represent Fire without a flame? How will you represent your deities and spirits if you can only choose from objects you find lying on the ground outside?

Temporarily put away all your usual magical tools and then try to reconstruct your sacred space using completely different objects. You may set your own parameters to challenge yourself to whatever degree you deem appropriate. Then, use your sacred space. Spend a lunar cycle, a season, or some other designated period of time working in this different environment. You can't help but learn new things and reinvigorate your foundational skills when required to throw out everything you know and start fresh!

Chapter 3
Devotion

I can remember the exact moment I experienced the gods for the first time. Rather, I can remember the moment that I unequivocally, overwhelmingly accepted the reality of the divine outside myself. Maybe they'd been there the whole time and I was only now hearing them. Maybe some magical something had finally clicked in my brain, and I suddenly became visible to them. Honestly, I go back and forth. I'd been Pagan since I was a young teenager. By this point, I'd explored several kinds of Witchcraft, though I was not yet an initiate in any tradition. I knew a fair bit about magic (at least in theory), and I'd certainly *read* a lot about gods and various kinds of spirits. But I was years into my practice before I was finally jolted into reality: I didn't know shit. Funnily enough, this profound, life-altering realization didn't come as the result of any grand act of Witchcraft. It didn't happen in the Wiccan-style circle I had grown accustomed to, nor did I hear a mysterious voice in the forest, have visions, or raise my yearning voice to the moon (I mean, I'd done that, but in these early days the results were questionable). Instead, it happened during a Vodou-inspired trance possession ritual at a Pagan festival—a ritual that I had been invited to by a new friend who had some inner impulse that said I should be there.[14]

At that point in my life, I had never seen anything like this ritual, which my companion told me was called a *fête*—a French word that means "party" or "celebration" on account of how practitioners entice the spirits to join them. A giant, elaborate altar was set up at the front of a run-down building that looked like it had once been a gymnasium. It was covered in objects that were sacred to the various spirits that would be invited that night: fans and beautiful yellow scarves for Oshun, fat cigars for Ogun, and copper bangles and a long multicolored skirt for Oya. Participants used cornstarch to draw complex symbols, called *veves*, representing each spirit, pouring them out precisely onto the wooden floor. As a ring of drummers played, dancers swirled, stomped, and spun across the space, their feet kicking up yellow dust. All night, offerings were made, songs were sung to invite each spirit individually, and some chosen devotees offered their bodies up to them so that they might enjoy drinks, food, dancing, and words with the people present.

An observing skeptic, armed as I was with a first-year sociology course under her belt and a passing knowledge of the work of Émile Durkheim, would attribute what I saw that night to collective effervescence, which is the phenomenon of large social groups energetically shifting together to create an atmosphere that sweeps individuals into a collective experience. If you've ever gone to a party and gotten caught up in the festive mood even though you were feeling tired or sad, or if you've watched as sports fans in a giant stadium all seem to lose their minds together during a game, you've seen collective effervescence in action. Durkheim (1858–1917), a famous French scholar and the long-celebrated father of the social sciences, described this phenomenon as a way of explaining religious fervor. Subsequently, this concept has been somewhat dismissively applied to religious experience as a whole. After all, in a large, hot

---

14. I say "Vodou-inspired" because Vodou is an initiatory religion with established histories and traditions. Most of the people present were not initiates, and this was a rite specifically for festival attendees, who may or may not have been practitioners (I certainly was not). For more about Vodou and other African Traditional Religions, I recommend the work of Lilith Dorsey.

room full of rhythmic drumming, singing, and insistent bodies, surely it was no great feat that a newcomer would be swept up in the atmosphere and begin to feel that something otherworldly was in fact afoot.

I certainly don't deny that collective effervescence plays a role in effective group ritual, but looking into the eyes of those being "horsed" by the spirits that night, I knew in my gut that there was more at work here. And, later in the night, when the woman who was embodying Oya—a woman whom I had never seen before, let alone spoken to—sought me out on the sidelines and spoke to me authoritatively about a personal matter she could not possibly have known about, I was so shaken I could have been sick then and there.

So are the gods real? Do spirits sometimes walk among us? Can our ancestral dead still speak? Yes, I know this to be true. I don't pretend to be a theologian, and I don't discount a scientific understanding of the world, but as a Witch—whose experiences of the otherworld became both more frequent and more intense after that night—I believe with my whole being that there are divine forces in the world that go beyond what so many of us expect. And, for many Witches, what we expect is actually quite modest. Plenty of spell books will tell you that magic and prayer are fundamentally about psychological manipulation: we change our attitudes, so we change our perceptions. It doesn't matter if the gods are real, only that our *belief* in them alters our interactions with the world. You'd better not hope for too much—beginner books and online reality exposés often warn us—because modern Witchcraft isn't spooky and dramatic the way it is in Hollywood and fairy tales.

Well, why not? We have hundreds of years' worth of history and folklore telling us that Witches communicate with the spirit world, the dead, the fae, and the old gods in order to work wonders. Billions of people throughout the world subscribe to religions in which gods speak to humans, either directly or through prophets. Even people who say they don't believe in magic or deities will often engage in magical cultural practices, such as "sending thoughts and prayers" to sick people, not labeling the thirteenth floor of buildings, or wearing lucky shirts to sporting events to support a favorite team. So what if we set our expectations a little higher than the power of positive thinking and excerpts from Émile Durkheim?

In this chapter, we'll explore the Witch's relationship with divine realities and otherworlds through an exploration of devotion, whether to the gods, to a body of spirits, to the land, or to your own development as a person. You don't have to believe as I do, and you don't need to experience the gods in any particular way. It is the epitome of hubris to declare that divinity only appears in certain forms, or even to say that it definitely exists in some prescribed way and not in others. There are many types of Witches, and many ways of working with gods, spirits, the mighty dead, the fae, land wights, and many more magical others unique to our various traditions. There are also Witches who describe themselves as atheists, secular, or otherwise non-religious, so there is nothing to say that you must experience divine or magical others at all. However, taking your Witchcraft to the next level, regardless of your specific beliefs or tradition (or lack of either) entails the conscious, deliberate decision to expect more from the world and to push the limits of what you assume through experience or social conditioning to be possible. It requires that you address the question of who you are and what you're doing with your life.

What Does It Mean to Be Devoted?

Devotion can be a triggering word for some, because, like *worship*, it seems to hearken back to the churches that so many Witches have worked to escape. One of the hallmarks of Witchcraft is freedom: freedom to define our own path, freedom to make our own choices, and freedom from oppression (and to fight it where it arises). Devotion seems to imply something else. Many of us hear the word and think of rules, extremism, or passivity in the face of something that claims superiority unjustly. To some extent, these associations are fair. Devotion always *requires* things of us: time, energy, effort, study, or commitment. Sometimes devotion requires money, as we may acquire books or tools, support local religious organizations (as when Christians tithe their income to their churches), pay to take classes, or save for travel to events or sacred places. While devotion should never be blind or passive, it is often difficult.

The word *devotion* comes from Latin via Old French and means to dedicate with a vow, to sacrifice oneself, or to consecrate something or someone, especially in the service of a deity. Like *sacred*, to devote is to set apart, and setting apart is rarely easy, especially when what we're setting apart is ourselves. It can be isolating, in that friends and family sometimes don't understand. It means more obligations—to people, causes, communities, and divine entities—and that necessarily leaves less time for more casual pursuits. It can get in the way of romantic relationships. It can also be painful, as when you experience judgment from others, or are required to carry out challenging personal tasks, especially when you can't quite explain them to onlookers. Consider that in many traditions around the world, devoted individuals—often priests or scholars of some sort—live apart from the rest of the community and do not engage in more mundane affairs.

So why on earth do people do it? Why on earth would a Witch—who perhaps should only be concerned with controlling their world through magic—choose to be *devoted*? In a world where it's so much easier to live purely for yourself and your immediate pleasures, why serve? Why set yourself aside?

Interestingly, the answer has little to do with your opinions on the exact nature of the gods or spirits and everything to do with the word *Witchcraft* itself. This is a *craft*—a thing that entails learning, practice, and *doing*.

Consider for a moment whether you've personally experienced this or not, the process of learning to play an instrument. As listeners of music, it's easy to enjoy a song on the radio or at a live performance and think, "Wow, that performer is really talented!" If we've never played the guitar before or never sung in front of an audience, we may have a hard time imagining the finer points of what goes into that performance. We only get to see the end result and are, if all goes well, impressed. We toss the word *talented* around because this, we're told, is the difference between the musician onstage and us laypeople watching from the audience.

What we don't see are the thousands of hours spent practicing. We don't see tedious scale runs, bleeding fingers and hoarse throats, the hundreds of not-so-spectacular performances, the thousands of dollars forked over first for lessons and then for music school. We don't see the years of social outings and relaxing evenings on the couch sacrificed for recitals and rehearsals, auditions, and recording sessions. We don't see the years of struggle that went into that one song, that one gig. Only the perfected final product. So is it really fair to say that the difference is talent? Raw ability is a boon, certainly, but the difference between mediocrity and greatness is labor and sacrifice, in practically any instance you could name, even where genius is involved.

This drive to be great is devotion. It's why the original Latin meaning of the word *passion* is "to suffer." We devote ourselves to a pursuit because of love and because of a desire for something beyond the ordinary. Perhaps we want to be like the deity in question, as Christians aspire to live like Christ. Perhaps we want to be great at something, like an instrument, an art form, dance, scholarship, or a sport. As Witches, we aspire to live unlike other people—to have stronger connections, more control in our lives, more opportunity, more access to power and knowledge. In many magical traditions, there is also the concept of the Great Work, ascension, or higher purpose. To accomplish these things—to live extraordinary lives—we must *practice*. We must work the *Craft* of the Witch.

Here, I'm calling that practice devotion. You must locate the core of your Craft and do the work that it requires. For most of us, that means building a relationship with the divine, connecting with our ancestral dead, communing with the land that supports our existence, or developing our personal spirits—our souls—so that we may live extraordinary lives rich in meaning.

God-Touched

Most varieties of Witchcraft, whether formal traditions or individual practices, have some conception of the gods, though what exactly that means may vary by quite a lot. Thanks to the influence of Margaret Murray, who published *The God of the Witches* in 1931, and Robert Graves, whose work *The White Goddess* had a far-reaching impact on magical communities of many kinds after it was released in 1948, Witches of many traditions speak of a goddess and a god. For early Wiccans, and subsequently today's traditional Wiccans, these are the Horned God of death, resurrection, wild places, and animals and his partner and lover-mother the Triple Goddess, whose symbol is the moon. She rules over lunar cycles, the tides, darkness, pleasure and reproduction, and the internal Mysteries of these initiatory traditions. The relationship between these two—from birth to maturation, sexual union to death and rebirth—is marked in the changing seasons, metaphorically (and sometimes literally) tied to agricultural cycles of planting and harvesting. Many Wiccans also tie this divine interplay to our own human bodies, celebrating the Goddess as she manifests as Maiden, Mother, and Crone. Men, meanwhile, may relate to the Horned God as he grows from the divine child at the winter solstice to his sexual prime at May Eve, and then to the wizened sage and eventually the lord of death in the autumn months. Wiccans also understand these cycles metaphorically, especially as we raise cultural questions surrounding gender norms and expectations, working with their personal energy levels, creative projects, and homelife in accordance with the turning of this, the Wheel of the Year.

For Wiccans, one of the most fundamental objectives of practice is to internalize these cycles and to build personal meaning around them. It doesn't matter per se whether a Wiccan sees these gods as literal, discrete entities, abstractions, archetypal representations, or as aspects of some supremely singular divine All. What matters is that we experience them in some meaningful way. This meaning-making is part of the collective work of the coven, but it also requires a great deal of work on the part of the individual. With so much variety, even among Witches in one coven, it is critical that we pursue our own experiences, ask our own questions, and arrive at perspectives (or at least pass through them) that feel like our own. After all, the coven meeting will eventually end, with each Witch left to return home. There should be meaning waiting upon arrival.

Non-Wiccan Witches, who seem in many spaces to increasingly outnumber Wiccans, are often heavily influenced by this model, despite other differences. Traditional Witches—so-called because of their connections to localized folklore and historical Witch trial records—sometimes work with a god of Witches, variously described as a god of blacksmithing, the forest, death, or even the devil of Christian mythology, depending on the specific working context. Many pair him with a goddess of Witches, who may be Lilith, Hecate, Babalon (hearkening to Aleister Crowley and the traditions of Thelema), and many more besides. As with any individualistic, decentralized movement, a wonderful amount of variation exists (and plenty of these non-Wiccan and Traditional Witches do not believe in gods at all, but we'll come to that in another section).

Beyond these two groups, there are many more Witches who simply define themselves as eclectic. Eclectic Witches may or may not belong to a particular tradition, but the term gained traction in the nineties with popular authors like Silver RavenWolf and DJ Conway, who were writing at a time when most Witches were learning and practicing outside of a coven structure. This may not sound revolutionary today, when the overwhelming majority of Witches are solitary, but this represented a significant shift in how people approached becoming Witches.[15] Previously, seekers were mostly reliant on contact with formal teachers and covens. But now, anyone could go to a chain bookstore or get online and teach themselves! Eclectic Witches were (and are) those who pull from multiple sources, teachers, and traditions to build their own practice, without being bound to set structures, lineages, or prescribed codes of conduct. Eclectic Witches may work with any number of gods, either devoting themselves entirely to one or two, or calling on several for different purposes.

As a Witch, these models and many more besides are available to you, depending on your desire to pursue a particular path, your natural inclinations, and the experiences you've had so far in your practice. Most Witches—no matter what type—will change their minds at some point, one way or another. Particular beliefs may suit us perfectly well at one point in our lives but then begin to feel cumbersome later on. If your practice is sincere and well-tended, it will grow and change as you learn and experience more.

---

15. In 2003, Evan A. Leach, Helen A. Berger, and Leigh S. Shaffer released *Voices from the Pagan Census: A National Survey of Witches and Neo-Pagans in the United States* from University of South Carolina Press. This report is somewhat dated, but the trends it demonstrates are nonetheless useful. Berger's *Solitary Pagans: Contemporary Witches, Wiccans, and Other Who Practice Alone* (Columbia: University of South Carolina Press, 2019) provides additional, more current insight.

Why Worship?

Like *religion*, the word *worship* is a term that many Witches avoid. Used casually, it seems to imply subservience. In the vernacular we tend to use it dismissively or to imply some kind of personal failure or grossness. In the movie *Practical Magic*, Nicole Kidman's character, Gillian, describes her abusive relationship as one in which she and her boyfriend "worship" each other, which worries her intervening sister (and cues the audience that this dude is a problem) because it emphasizes the destructive power dynamic at play. Culturally, we speak of "hero worship" in children but also in impressionable, misled adults, who are misplacing their adoration for someone who does not deserve it. We also criticize consumers for "worshipping" money or fashion. In each of these examples, personal sacrifice is the result of poor judgment, abuse, or naïveté. No wonder so many spiritual people cringe at the word, when these are the examples we have! Finally, and perhaps most prevalently, most of us have been exposed (and overexposed) to vocal evangelical communities and individuals whose worship practices are coupled with prejudice and violence aimed at outsiders and dissenters. These kinds of negative associations are reason enough for many to shy away from both the term and the practice itself. However, it's well worth going deeper and questioning whatever baggage you may have attached here.

Taken at face value, most definitions of worship simply point to reverence, being in awe, or offering dramatic praise, and these are all things that I do in relation to my gods. None of those things necessarily belittles my value or compromises my autonomy or my decision-making abilities. I revere my gods—I am in awe of them—because of the depth of feeling that encounters with them inspire. Like love, I simply cannot help it. I have been struck silent and moved to tears during ritual invocation to the divine, and so much of my personal practice is about the pursuit of those often fleeting moments. The space in between those moments can be difficult. That's when life can get in the way or depression robs me of the memory of the divine. It's also when my intellectual, rational side can persuade me that I am only fabricating these experiences. But when I am in circle, I am ultimately working to touch something beyond myself, and to pull it down and carry it with me when I leave. Doing so makes me *better*, not lesser. While some Witches choose to say that they "partner" with the gods, or that they "work with" a particular deity, this language does not adequately express my own experiences. I may be an expression of the divine, and I may have the capacity to transcend myself, but I am not there yet. I am *of* the gods, but not myself a god.

For some Witches, worship is about reciprocity. We worship the gods because they *want* to be worshipped, and in exchange they bless us, comfort us, grant us special abilities, or teach us. Our rituals are an exchange of energy—as we give to the gods, so the gods give to us. Under this model, you might seek out a relationship with a particular god because they possess qualities that you desire, or because you wish to learn one of their skills, or otherwise to petition them for help in some area of your life. In exchange, you might give specific offerings, perform special rituals, spread the knowledge of that god to others so that their influence grows, or fight for causes that are meaningful to that god. This kind of reciprocal divine relationship is often where people start, and it can be a good way to build a foundation, but it must deepen beyond this in order to remain viable. After all, life will inevitably become difficult, and the gods—whatever your perception of them—will not shield you from suffering at every turn. If your worship is entirely about *getting*—material blessings, luck, smooth sailing through life—where does that leave you when life goes awry? There are many gods in the world and many ways to approach them, but none of them are vending machines. You rarely can simply say a prayer and leave an offering and have your wishes granted without question. Worship must be rooted in love, first, and that love is usually born out of ritual experience or other direct encounters. The possibility of those encounters is what drives devotion.

Patron Deities

Wherever you are in your own relationship with gods, a common piece of advice is to begin with a patron (or sometimes a "matron," for a goddess, though linguistically these terms are not interchangeable and have distinct origins—a patron is a supporter or protector, whereas a matron is a household position, or an older married woman). There is a fair bit of heated discussion in Witchcraft and polytheist communities as to how exactly one acquires a patron deity. Many will say that it is the gods who must choose you. Some even claim that the gods choose us at birth, and coming to them is a process of awakening. By being a certain kind of person or having certain kinds of experiences or affinities, you are more inclined to attract and relate to some deities versus others. A writer or a scholar may be called to the scribe god Thoth, for example, whereas a soldier may be drawn to the Morrigan. Other practitioners believe that we can choose freely, based on interest or what we desire to draw into our lives in the moment. These Witches may choose Aphrodite as a patron, because they wish to learn the mysteries of love and draw it to them, or Frigga, as they establish a household and tend to children.

Is one perspective inherently better or more correct than the other? Some will criticize those who appear to treat the gods as mere correspondences, interchanging them to suit a particular spell. At the same time, who has the hubris to declare definitively that they can speak for a god— that they alone know what is truly proper and required? Some will insist that approaching a god improperly could actually put you in danger, and yet people do so all the time, seemingly without consequence (I tend to think that gods are too busy with more important things to punish the oversights of sincere spiritual explorers).

If you have not already, you must explore and reach your own understanding alone. After years of practice, it is very likely that your experiences will change your perspectives, whatever they may be now. There is merit, and also overlap, to both approaches. After all, your interests and experiences will likely attract particular deities, as you will likely be attracted to them.

If you are new to the concept of patron deities, or perhaps are simply interested in beginning a relationship with a new deity, try the following exercise, which is part research and part ritual:

Pretend that you are going to host a dinner party with a god as the guest of honor. This could be practically any deity at this point: one you're curious about, one you've met and are trying to establish a relationship with, or one you've been pursuing for years but who remains mysterious (which, let's be real, is plenty of them).

Your task is to assemble a menu, choose a venue, and make a guest list. You can be as creative and far-reaching as you want here—we are engaging in spiritual play. Will it be a large event or intimate? What foods will be welcome and which taboo? Is there anyone you'd better make sure *doesn't* show up? Will you let the conversation flow on its own, or should you plan party games and other entertainment? What should guests wear? If gifts are involved, what would be appropriate? If you were going to put together a registry, what would be on it? Remember: this is not about what *you* would prefer. This is for the deity. It's easy to lean on your own preferences and habits, but force yourself to really think about and research what *they* would want (or not want).

When you've imagined and recorded as many details as possible, use what you've accumulated to actually make a formal toast to the god in question. You may choose to erect an altar, either temporary or permanent, and decorate it with the things (or symbols and images of the things) you came up with in your planning. Make or acquire one of the foods or beverages on your menu and present it as an offering. Invite the deity to partake, offer favorable words, and then ask them to stay or perhaps to demonstrate interest in a relationship with you. This need not be an elaborate or mysterious process: you can write poetry, or you can speak simply. Afterward, you will look for signs, note your impressions and feelings, and follow your intuition. Your final task is to decide what to actually do with the food or drink you used! Should you consume it yourself? Bury it? Pour it in running water? Feed it to animals? What would be most appropriate based on what you've learned?

This exercise may result in a new relationship or not, but in either case you will have learned something.

Devotion isn't only about gods. It's easy to forget that, because deities are at the fore of so many conversations about Witchcraft. Your practice may or may not include gods, but you can still be devoted as a Witch. For many practitioners of various traditions, devotion manifests through a relationship with ancestral spirits, which we will discuss next.

Where We Come From

Ancestor veneration is an integral part of many religious and cultural traditions. Both Catholics and Buddhists may pray or conduct rituals to aid dead loved ones, negotiating existence in the afterlife (whether to escape purgatory or to be freed from the cycle of birth and rebirth). In some Chinese traditions, living family members may burn special joss paper printed to look like currency, and often called "hell money," for family members to use in the afterlife, which is thought to be as bureaucratic as this one. Throughout the world, parents name children after long-passed relatives and preserve memories in inherited recipes, prized possessions, and extensive photo albums. Americans in particular—perhaps because so many of us are immigrants, are part of diaspora communities, or have experienced displacement—are often fiercely interested in heritage and genealogy, happily asserting distant connections to royalty, the early colonies, or some historic moment of particular significance. Many pay money and swab their cheeks to collect DNA for analysis in the hopes of discovering an answer to the foundational question of "Where did I come from?"

Why do we care so much? Well, for lots of reasons. Primarily, we all seem to have a fundamental need to connect to others in order to build meaning in our lives, and exploring our ancestry is a way to do this. Knowing more about where we came from potentially tells us something about where we're going, what we've overcome, and what sort of person we could become. On a magical level, many traditions teach that we carry ancestral memories, perhaps lurking in the makeup of our cells or else stored in the collective unconscious, as described by thinkers like Carl Jung. Learning about our familial and cultural past can be a beautiful and powerful way to feed our present. For some, this is much easier than for others. In the United States, there is no overlooking the legacy of slavery, which has denied many Black Americans knowledge of their ancestry past a few generations. Practitioners who are adopted or who are alienated from their families of origin may have even more limited genealogical knowledge. Some of us have the luxury and privilege of clear family lineages, whereas others may only have access to their most immediate families.

For many Witches, their ancestors represent a potent connection to other worlds and sources of power. In the same way that having a large network among the living can provide you with support, resources, opportunities, and many other benefits besides, having a network among the dead may do the same. As in your day-to-day life, people with a personal investment in your well-being tend to be more likely to want to act on your behalf than strangers do. For many of us, that means our families! All over the world, people of myriad traditions turn to their direct genetic ancestors for guidance and support. For some, as for gods, this relationship is one of reciprocity. We provide our dead with offerings, remembrance, praise, and work their desires in the world of the living, and in exchange they grant us blessings, protection, or wisdom from beyond the veil. For others, ancestral veneration is not about what we can *get* but what we can give. We celebrate and honor them out of love or out of the need to offer healing to those who may have died with emotional or spiritual wounds. If a Witch believes in reincarnation, as many do, then eventually our beloved dead may go on to be born again, and our working with them may serve to help them progress faster, to live happier lives, and to heal from wrongs that were done unto them or that they themselves perpetuated while alive. Many Witches believe that when we heal ourselves, we also heal our bloodlines.

Blood family, however, as most anyone can tell you, isn't the only kind of family, and your ancestors aren't only the people contributing to your personal makeup. For many Witches, a relationship with their direct biological ancestors could actually be harmful because of past traumas and deep emotional wounds. It's okay not to want anything to do with the people you're related to. The truth is many other people may have gone into making you the person you are today, whether or not they were biological relatives, and those who have died can be counted among your ancestors as well. They may even be *more* important to you. As a Wiccan initiate, for example, I possess a lineage of high priestesses and high priests through which I trace both magical power and authority within my specific tradition. Some of these are people I've never met, and none are people I'm connected to through blood, but they nonetheless represent a kind of family for me. I honor them in ritual, and I think of them as my spiritual ancestors, and these are just as important to me. I also include Witches who, though they may not be a part of this upline or even my tradition, were extraordinarily influential in guiding me on my path, however from a distance. Scott Cunningham and Raven Grimassi hold places of honor on my ancestral shrine, because of the immense impact they've had in my life, alongside Doreen Valiente, Gerald Gardner, and Ray Buckland. I never met most of these people, but their work helped make me who and what I am.

Whoever and wherever you are, you are connected to others. As an exercise, take out a sheet of paper and begin listing those who have died who had a hand in your life. You may choose to divide them into columns according to whether they are biological family, adopted family, friends, spiritual guides, figures from history, or your professional life who have inspired you, or even animals you may have loved and lost. If you have a spiritual lineage, trace it as far back as you can. Who influenced the people who influenced you? Finally, make a family tree. Begin with your parents (biological or not, however many parents you have) and go as far back as possible. You may find some surprises!

Once you've made your lists and assembled as much of your family tree as possible, choose the people whom you feel closest to or, conversely, whom you didn't know well or at all and wish to learn about. You may want to build a separate altar where you keep symbols or mementos of those ancestors. Build relationships through conversation, prayer, and offerings (perhaps the person's favorite snacks, fresh flowers, favorite beverages, bowls of clear water, reading aloud from a favorite book, or playing cherished music).

As with gods, establishing and developing meaningful ancestral relationships can be slow and will often require special attention to subtle signs, rather than fireworks. A strong tie to the ancestral realm is the cornerstone of many Witchcraft practices. Indeed, for many Witches, the essential function and purpose of the Craft is the ability to communicate with the dead, both to aid the living and those who are struggling in the afterlife. Many nontheistic Witches emphasize an ancestral practice, while others work with the dead in addition to their work with gods. In either case, adopting a devotional practice centered upon your ancestors can do much to inform and expand your experiences as a Witch.

The Land

More fundamental than our beloved dead or the gods we may serve, there is the earth itself. Indeed, for many Witches it is the land they live on that is the foundation of their entire practice. Without it, we could not survive, so what could be more important? Here too is a thing worthy of a Witch's devotion and magical attention.

Many of us, myself included, came to Witchcraft under the impression that it was, at its core, a nature religion. As a youngster eagerly exploring Wicca in the nineteen-nineties, I read over and over again in popular books that becoming a Wiccan was about building a spiritual connection to the natural world and finding the faces of the Goddess and God in the turning of the seasons and the Wheel of the Year. The phrase *earth-based religion* was tossed around wantonly, like we could all just safely rest in the knowledge that to be a Pagan or a Witch (especially a Wiccan Witch) was to be an environmentalist.

Wasn't I surprised to find out over the years that that wasn't necessarily the case? Yes, it is typical for all kinds of Witches to espouse the importance of nature, but what exactly does that mean? The Wiccan sabbats are based on agricultural festivals that aren't applicable for many practitioners who live in very different climates, don't farm or raise animals, and can't immediately translate those seasonal symbols and metaphors into their own lives. Meanwhile, the majority of us learn about animal magic, crystals and minerals, and herbalism using specimens that have been collected, hunted, mined, and harvested from hundreds or even thousands of miles away, and often under ethically questionable circumstances. We happily collect beautifully cut and polished crystals from Brazil, Madagascar, Afghanistan, and elsewhere, but we can rarely recognize the minerals that may be equally precious under our feet. We look to animal guides and oracle decks that romanticize wolves, bears, stags, eagles, and other widely recognizable, impressive animals, when we may never have the opportunity to encounter them in real life. Meanwhile we often have no sense of the animals that make their homes in our own backyards.

I'm guilty of this myself, so this isn't me throwing stones at you. I think it's something a lot of us come to realize eventually and have to handle in some way. Can we truly say we're engaging with nature when our experience of nature is so often prepackaged, romanticized, and marketed to us like any other product we could buy? We can even see this in the language we use: nature is a thing we strive to "get back to," "get away to," or "discover," as though it isn't already all around us and part of us. Paradoxically, when we pursue our "earth-based religion," we're often isolating ourselves further, just in different ways.

There's a lot to lose when this is our only relationship with the natural world. When nature is elsewhere—only in remote forests and untouched oceans or deserts—we miss out on what is around us. Whether you live in a giant city, a developed suburb, or the ideal Witch's cottage in some private wood, there is land under your feet, sky above you, and plant and animal life all around you. When we don't appreciate that, it's easier to be insensitive to the needs of our own environment. It's easier to tacitly allow their misuse and even to participate in that misuse ourselves. The root of our collective crises with climate change, mass extinction, and pollution isn't *hatred* for the natural world—most of us aren't contributing to these awful things maliciously—but *indifference*. We are separated from the natural world on a cultural level, and this manifests in our spiritual and magical practices.

Aside from all that, as Witches we're also just missing out on magical opportunities when we ignore our own surroundings for some distant Arcadia. Imagine being able to heal, to cast, and to contact the spirit world using plants that you forage from your own neighborhood. Imagine drawing power from the stones under your feet, rather than budgeting for expensive crystals imported from halfway around the world. Imagine finding allies among the animal spirits right outside your window. You would never be alone or without resources.

Given our often tenuous personal relationships with our immediate environment, it may be unfair to call Witchcraft "nature-based" as a whole. Your particular tradition may not even aspire to such things, as is the case for many practitioners of more ceremonial traditions of Witch-craft. However, a devotional practice centered upon the land is at the very core of many, and this is a worthy pursuit for many an advancing Witch. In getting to know the specific place that sustains you, you may discover it has its own deities, its own spirits, and its own innate power. Even if you are neither theist nor animist, there is profound meaning and purpose in spending time in the nature that surrounds you and perhaps becoming a caretaker of it. Imagine how the world might change if every Witch came to love the land that immediately sustained them and took it upon them-selves to serve its well-being.

Learning the Land

How does one go about beginning a devotional practice to the land? Most of us aren't naturalists, after all, and it's often no small matter to simply disappear into some wood and instantly feel at home. Nor do you have to! For this exercise, you may not even need to leave your home, except per-haps to visit the library. You'll come to spend more time outside as your practice develops, but some of what you'll learn here would be impossible to learn through observation alone. You're going to have to dig a bit.

Research and record the answers to the following questions. Some of these you may already know, but there are sure to be many that hold sur-prises for you:

1. How many names have been given to the land you live on? What do the locals call it? How is it designated on maps? Does it have names bestowed by the peoples who lived here before you and your ancestors? Try to find at least five.

2. Who first inhabited this land? Who settled it and when? Was it colonized? What people still live here?

3. What is the climate like? How is it classified, scientifically? Has that changed at any point?

4. What natural resources have historically been harvested here? What, if anything, do people farm, mine, hunt, or otherwise pro-duce for consumption here today?

5. Where does the water you drink come from? Trace the water cycle from source to tap.

6. Where does the food in your grocery store come from? Is any of it produced locally? Is there a farmer's market or other source of local foods available to you?

7. How much garbage does your community produce each year, and where does it go? If you participate in a recycling program, where do recyclables go and how are they processed?

8. Name five species of native birds. For each, describe its migratory and breeding pattern, its food source, and its predators. Which species appear first as the seasons change, and which are the first to migrate elsewhere?

9. Name five species of edible native plants. Where might you find them, and how might you prepare them?

10. Name five species of native trees, shrubs, or grasses. How would you recognize them? Are any of them edible? Toxic? What are their life cycles?

11. Name five species of either plants or animals that have gone extinct in your region within the last 100 years. Why did they go extinct?

12. Is hunting or fishing allowed in your area? How is it regulated? What animals do people pursue, and when are their seasons? How does hunting and fishing impact the local ecosystem?

13. What reptiles and amphibians live here? Are any of them venomous? Are any of them endangered?

14. What plants and animals have been introduced in your area? How do they impact the local ecosystem? Are there any eradication efforts underway?

15. Name five species of insects and arachnids that are native. Be specific. How would you recognize them from similar species?

16. Name five non-domesticated animals that might share your home, whether or not you're aware of it. Are they destructive or helpful? How might you deter or encourage them?

These questions are a starting place only, but they will give you a much better than average grasp of the relationships at work on the land around you. You will, of course, then have to get out there and discover what you can face-to-face! You may develop a newfound love for birding, gardening, foraging, hunting, community cleanup, wildlife rehabilitation, and many other things besides. Any could become essential to your personal practice of Witchcraft.

The Sacred Self

There are many Witches today who are not theists. Many do not maintain a practice of ancestor veneration. Many are not called to the caretaking of the land and are not even environmentalists. These Witches may describe themselves as secular or non-religious, or they may simply have no term at all. There is no requirement in Witchcraft that a practitioner worship (or even believe in) gods or serve any particular set of spirits. You'll recall from chapter 1 that my own working definition of Witchcraft entailed three criteria: the transgression of boundaries, the practice of magic, and interaction with the spirit world. It's that last one that would seem to be a stumbling block here. If not gods, the dead, or the spirits of the land and its fauna and flora, then what? Why practice Witchcraft if there is no outside force that warrants our devotion? Well, because Witchcraft also serves to expand and develop something even more foundational than anything we've discussed so far: you! Your body houses its own spirit, and its tending is as worthy a devotional practice as any.

For many Witches, their practice is specifically rooted in an ethic of personal development. Consider how many books have come out in recent years focusing on Witchcraft as an act of self-care or as a therapeutic endeavor in which practitioners master their "shadows" and come out the other side as empowered, self-actualized, and confident in their identities. Many take up the mantle of the Witch out of a longing to connect with the self—to reclaim power in the face of oppression, or to fulfill a personal calling. When we become Witches, we can come to know and love ourselves as we truly are. Through the acquisition of knowledge and power, we better ourselves and improve the depth and quality of our lives.

These ideas are today relegated to the realm of "self-help" or "personal development" when we discuss them in mixed company and when we go seeking them on bookstore shelves, but they have been a cornerstone of occult practice for well over a hundred years. In the mid-nineteenth century classic *Transcendental Magic: Its Doctrine and Ritual* by Éliphas Lévi, the central focus for the magician is the achievement of the Great Work, which is actually a chain of achievements: the philosophical stone (or philosopher's stone, more commonly), the universal medicine, the transmutation of metal, the quadrature of the circle, and the secret of perpetual motion. The mastery of magic entails the granting of certain powers and privileges, each corresponding to one of the Hebrew letters. These include the power to conquer both love and hate, to live above fear, to know the future, and to behold God face to face. In short, to master the self to such an extent that pain, death, and even the armies of heaven are unable to touch the magus who wields them.[16]

Other occultists, magicians, and Witches have understood the Great Work to be the soul's reunion with the divine, the ascension of the human form into godhead. In some traditions, the Great Work is the quest to converse with one's personal Holy Guardian Angel, which is variously a pure, external force, or some inner genius or aspect of the magician's personality. Aleister Crowley tells us in *Magick Without Tears* that "the Great Work is the uniting of opposites. It may mean the uniting of the soul with God, of the microcosm with the macrocosm, of the female with the male, of the ego with the non-ego."[17] Other magicians and Witches liken the Great Work with the quest for the Holy Grail.

From any angle, the Great Work is essentially about the personal, individual development of the magician. For many contemporary Witches, though we may use different language, this focus is equally present. Being a Witch may or may not be about serving gods or building relationships with spirits and other external forces, but it is always about nurturing your own power and growing into a masterful, attuned person. For many, that means claiming lost power: learning to stand up for yourself,

---

16. Éliphas Lévi, *Transcendental Magic: Its Doctrine and Ritual*, trans. Arthur Edward Waite (London: Bracken Books, 1995), 13–14.

17. Aleister Crowley, *Magick Without Tears* (Scottsdale, AZ: New Falcon Press, 1991), 7.

to fight injustice on behalf of yourself or others, or to otherwise survive and thrive in a harsh world. For others, Witchcraft is a tool to explore the psyche: to come to terms with personal traumas and destructive patterns, to build empathy, and to embrace one's emotions and personal quirks (or to change them as desired). Many are attracted to Witchcraft because it can help practitioners develop self-love, as well as a sense of gratitude. Through Witchcraft, the body—which so many of us learn to abhor from a young age—becomes sacred and worthy of the utmost care, and this can be a life-changing experience, especially for people with marginalized bodies. On a more practical level, the craft of the Witch—herbalism, energy work, the making of charms, and much more—may be a significant force of healing, prosperity, love, and growth in our mundane lives. You may find that your devotional work as a Witch is closely tied to the healing arts, which is the case for many Witches.

Witchcraft is a vessel through which we can change our lives, and this may be completely independent of gods or external spirits, or it may be integrally linked with worship and service. Most Witches practice some combination of the perspectives we've discussed in this chapter, though you should not allow any one to limit you. The key is to know the *why* behind your practice, and then allow that why to drive you forward. When you hit a rut, or when you don't know where to go next, it is always worth reexamining what lies at the heart of your Craft. Whether it is a deity, your ancestors, the land, or your sacred self, an attitude of devotion will serve you well. In the following exercise, we'll look at how to begin cultivating (or perhaps rediscovering) that perspective.

• EXERCISE •
Living a Devoted Life

These exercises are designed to foster a greater sense of devotion in your practice, regardless of your specific beliefs in the moment. Some ask you to connect with gods and spirits, while others push you to reflect on yourself. Few people maintain the exact same understanding of the sacred throughout their entire lives, so allow yourself space here to explore something new and potentially get uncomfortable. It's okay to feel like you're just playing pretend for now or to modify some of these to reflect your own worldview. You may choose to explore a theistic devotional practice and then conclude that it isn't for you. You may want to meet your ancestors and then decide never to speak to them again. The important thing is that you center your Witchcraft on something that is deeply meaningful to you.

Air

Many newcomers to Witchcraft get caught up with questions about gods and spirits, especially if they've come from other religious traditions. Do you have to pick a patron right away? Do you have to work with your ancestors even if you don't like them? Do you need to become an environmentalist or stop using animal products? Is any of this even real? It's easy to feel overwhelmed. If you need a way to orient yourself as you move forward and as you approach devotion—especially for the first time—root yourself in your core values. The things that are most important to you—the principles by which you live your life –will also guide you as you build and develop your practice as a Witch.

You probably already have some idea about what some of your core values are. If you've never really thought about it or haven't checked in with yourself recently, this exercise will pull those ideas to the fore and help you to make choices moving forward. If you know what you stand for, it is easier to answer the tough questions you'll face in your personal and spiritual development. As you have spirit encounters or explore deeper theological questions, you will continually be able to check those experiences against your innermost values and priorities.

You'll need your notebook and some journaling time! Begin by considering the list of concepts below. Read them all (and add more, if you note any important ones missing) and choose the ten that you value the most in your own life. If you're unsure, consider which of these you find most appealing in other people. Make your choices, and then write them in your notebook.

Abundance	Freedom	Perseverance
Adventure	Fun	Posterity
Ambition	Heritage	Power
Art	History	Practicality
Autonomy	Honesty	Recognition
Balance	Humanity	Religion
Beauty	Humility	Responsibility
Challenge	Humor	Security
Comfort	Inclusiveness	Self-control
Community	Individuality	Self-expression
Conservation	Influence	Service
Cooperation	Innovation	Sharing
Courage	Joy	Storytelling
Creativity	Justice	Strength
Curiosity	Knowledge	Success
Dedication	Learning	Thoughtfulness
Diversity	Love	Tradition
Ecology	Magic	Trust
Efficiency	Money	Truth
Empathy	Music	Understanding
Excellence	Nature	Wealth
Excitement	Optimism	Well-being
Fairness	Passion	Wisdom
Faith	Patience	
Family	Peace	

Once you've chosen the ten words that speak most to your personal values, cut that list in half. If you had to choose only five of those things to characterize the rest of your life, what would they be? Draw a line through the five that don't make the cut. Next, eliminate two more.

This may feel very difficult! You can use whatever rationale makes sense to you, but you should be left with only three. These represent or relate directly to your core values.

Now that you have your three words, we're going to do some reflecting on them. You can keep writing on the same sheet of paper, or add your thoughts to a magical journal or book of shadows:

1. Why did you choose these three words above all the others?

2. Describe at least one moment in your life when you exemplified these values (you may write about one when each was present or one moment for each, totaling three). How did you feel, and what were the consequences?

3. Describe a moment when these values were absent. How did you feel, and what were the consequences?

4. Where are these values present in your Witchcraft? What can you do to make them more central to your practice?

Your task moving forward is to consider your answers and then work to bring your core values to the fore of your practice as a Witch. Other types of devotional work may come later, but for now, let us begin by ensuring that the things that are already so core to your identity are at the heart of things.

Fire

One of the easiest, fastest ways to foster a devotional practice is through the use of daily devotions. In fact, if you've been practicing Witchcraft or another magical art for a while, it's likely that you've tried this before, or at least have read repeatedly that you should. Well, I'm here to tell you again! Daily devotions really are a game changer. They create space during the day where you return your thoughts to your central purpose, and this in turn provides you with perspective and support when things get tough or you start to feel disconnected. Some Witches have devotionals throughout the day, especially upon rising and before going to bed. Some practice routine meditation, affirmations, or even full rituals to reinforce the connections they've built in their practice. Like vowing to get off the couch and go to a gym, however, the mistake comes with promising too much too soon and setting unrealistic expectations. If you're like most people who've struggled with daily devotions, it's probably because you got a little too ambitious, too quickly.

Here, you'll come up with a devotional statement that you can use reliably every day. The nature of that devotional statement, of course, depends on the object of your devotion! If you are seeking to build a connection with a deity or with an ancestor, that statement may be a prayer. If you are focusing instead on yourself or on your relationship with the land, it may be more akin to an affirmation, in which you state an intention for yourself or your relationship with the world, rendering it true over time.

For years, I thought that prayer and affirmations were silly, uncomfortable, or just holdovers from other religions or from self-help communities that weren't really useful as a Witch. Now, however, I've developed a series of affirmations that I recite as a mantra, seated at my altar every morning. Some affirmations are about my connection to my gods ("I hear the voice of the gods and remain aware of them throughout the day"), while others are about my personal power ("I traverse freely in other realms") or about how I see myself ("I am healthy and confident"). I felt silly at first, but this ritual has expanded over the years and has really impacted my daily routine. I light a candle, I meditate for a few minutes, and I also practice divination in the form of a daily card draw. When I don't do these things, I feel it hard.

Your task is to come up with one devotional statement and to do it every day, at the same time of day, for one month. That's it. You don't have to light candles, stand outside (though if you're looking to build your connection to the natural world, this will help), or ritualize this any more than absolutely necessary. The point is that it's easy and attainable. Write your statement based on what is important to you in your devotional practice. Here are some examples:

For a deity or spirit:
- "I honor [spirit's name] this day and ask to feel their presence in my life."

- "I dedicate myself to [spirit's name] and ask to grow in their service."
- "May I always be reminded of my oaths to [spirit's name]."

For the land:
- "I am a part of this land and promise to be a caretaker of all who live here."
- "I hear the voice of nature and heed its call."
- "I commit myself to learning the land I inhabit."

For your personal development:
- "I am beautiful and confident as I move through the world."
- "I have strong boundaries and respect myself as I respect others."
- "I am a powerful Witch who grows in strength every day."

Note that all these statements are in the present tense and only include affirmative words like *do*, *will*, or *can*, as opposed to *don't*, *won't*, or *can't*. Speaking them as though they are already true, even if they aren't, conditions your mind to accept them as reality. You may use any of these or write your own, in accordance with your own practice and your own goals.

This tiny action can alter the tone of your day. It might sound far-fetched, but if you don't believe me, try doing this for one month, and then stop for a week. You'll feel the difference! On a practical level, speaking of something repeatedly brings it to the fore of your mind and will build that feeling of connection in your practice. On a magical level, speaking something repeatedly into the world causes it to manifest. The universe, the spirits, the dead, and the gods can all hear you.

Water

When it comes to devotion, depth comes when we build strong relationships, whether with ourselves or with outside entities. This exercise is modified from one that I've used within my own coven for years. We call it the God Project, but really it's applicable whether your focus is a deity, an ancestral or land spirit, or even your own personal spirit. It is a simple enough project, but in order to get the most out of it, you will need to take your time and really be as thorough as possible. You're going to spend some time intently getting to know and then ritually interacting with a deity or spirit. If you are already working with someone specific, you may choose them, but if you are interested in trying something different, or if you are entirely new to this sort of experience, you will now make a choice! Don't worry—this relationship does not need to be permanent. You won't be swearing any oaths!

If you are interested in working with a god, you may choose one that interests you or that you already have some sort of connection to. If you are feeling brave, or would like to incorporate some basic bibliomancy into this process, you might also find a guidebook to mythology and choose by opening to a random page (it sounds flippant, but I've seen students do this and have great success)! If you are interested in connecting with an ancestral spirit, you may choose a blood relation, someone from your spiritual lineage, or someone whose life has otherwise impacted your own. If your objective is to connect with the land, perhaps choose the spirit of a favorite tree or river. And of course, if you are interested in making your personal development the focus of your Witchcraft, then the obvious choice would be yourself!

You will spend the next month intently exploring this one entity, from a devotional perspective. At the beginning of the month, ritually declare your intentions and ask the god or spirit to allow you to get to know them. Do this in whatever manner feels right to you (you might even use the ritual from earlier in this chapter in which you planned a dinner party, modified however you need to). Afterward, research that spirit! Are there sacred texts associated with them? Are there myths to learn or rituals that have been performed historically to honor them? Are there family stories you could ask for from relatives or people who knew them? If your quest is to know yourself, consider working with a counselor or therapist to learn more about your personality and gain additional mastery over your behavior and thoughts. If you are working with the land, you will have already done much of this work with the Learning the Land exercise. Can you take those questions farther?

Set up an altar for the spirit you've chosen (even if it's yourself) and engage with it each day. At the end of the month, you will design and perform a ritual for that entity based on what you've discovered. Over the course of this period, it's possible that you will discover an intense connection that you wish to continue and develop. You may also discover that you are not well-matched at all, as in the case of a god or ancestral spirit. Your final ritual may be one of thanks and farewells, or it may be a resounding hello and a request for more! You may also find that a month is not enough time. The nature of the ritual is up to you, but you should design it yourself and perform it sincerely. (Don't stress if you're new to ritual work—simply turn to the next chapter!) Record your experiences, feelings, and afterthoughts in your journal or book of shadows.

Earth

It's natural to get into devotional ruts if you've been at this for a while. Perhaps you've experienced difficulties that have caused you to question your long-held traditions. Sometimes the passage of time just makes us forget who we are. Sometimes the divine seems silent, as though we've been cut off. We contemplate leaving, dismantling our sacred spaces, getting rid of our tools, and walking away from our communities. Few of us speak openly of these feelings, but plenty of us have had them, myself included. In other religions, there is the concept of the dark night of the soul, in which believers are driven to the brink by despair, disconnection, or trauma. It seems to be true that when life gets rough, spiritual practice is often one of the first things to go and one of the last to return. What do we do when this is where we find ourselves?

First, and most importantly, it's okay to feel stuck, uninspired, or depressed about your connection to your spirituality. There's nothing wrong with you, and those feelings are valid, even if, like me, you're the sort to beat yourself up over having them. Often, from this position it can seem like we only have two options: to quit or to press on and just hope things get better. For this exercise, however, we're going to explore a middle road. It's illogical to press forward exactly as you have been and expect change, but setting your practice down entirely may cause further spiraling, and make it more difficult to pick back up in the future. Instead, we're going to shift our focus elsewhere.

For the next month, you're going to explore and work within another tradition. As a beginner, you may have already explored other types of Witchcraft or Paganism before settling where you are now, but you are a different person than you were when you were first getting started. You may be surprised by how things appeal to you differently later in life. If you are an eclectic Witch, or have otherwise carved your own path, think of this as an opportunity to apply some outside structure for added support as you remind yourself why you chose the path you did in the first place. You may find that you like learning within a new framework!

You also do not need to choose another tradition of Witchcraft. You may explore a non-Witch style of Paganism or explore an entirely non-magical or non-occult tradition. When I found myself struggling to connect with the divine several years ago, I took enormous inspiration from attending a small, progressive Christian church that some friends of mine belonged to. I was never a Christian and did not want to become one, but I thought it was beautiful to see how they connected with God and brought the message of their faith into their daily lives. It fueled my Craft in surprising ways, but only because I was open enough to allow it to do so. (I was not raised in a Christian household, as many Witches were, and so I did not have the emotional wounds that so many carry—this situation would not have been nearly so useful or healthy for Witches with trauma surrounding churches.)

Choose another tradition based on whatever criteria you like, perhaps one that is closely related to what you already practice or perhaps an ancestral tradition. If you have friends who belong to other traditions, consider asking them to guide you. If you are a Traditional Witch, consider another tradition that also values ancestral work or nature, like Druidry. Traditional Wiccans may benefit from seeking out their local body of the Ordo Templi Orientis and attending a Gnostic Mass. Eclectic Witches might enjoy exploring a specific pantheon of deities. There are many magical traditions aside from Witchcraft. Perhaps ceremonial magic or a local brand of folk magic would appeal to you. If you have been working with a specific deity within the context of Witchcraft, consider their tradition of origin, if they have one. You may discover a love for historical reconstruction! Allow yourself to be surprised.

If you don't have a friend or contact who can guide you, choose a book to begin. If there is a group nearby, seek them out. Keep a journal while you learn about this new practice, and reflect on how it is different from what you've done in the past. Remember, this is only for the sake of widening your lens. You are not being asked to take any oaths or make any commitment beyond initial, sincere exploration. You may be re-inspired and happily return to your tradition of origin, but you may find a genuine calling elsewhere, and this is not something to fear. And if you really don't like what you've chosen, it's only one month! Allow yourself to learn from those who are different from you.

Chapter 4
Ritual and Magic

Lots of us come to Witchcraft for the spells. Hopefully, we go on to discover something deeper that makes a lifelong impact and totally changes how we engage with the world, but it's the ability to do magic that's the big draw for a lot of us. When I first started reading about the Craft, a big part of the appeal for me was the thought of performing mysterious rituals. What would it be like to wait for the fall of night, to fill a room with lit candles, and then to chant in a secret language to some arcane power? And then to know that it had a real effect out in the world (or in my case, school, where I routinely felt like I had no power at all)?

Magic and ritual are deeply intertwined. Considered broadly, it would be very difficult to separate one from the other entirely as, even where the individual Witch might perform one without the other, they are often cultivated together. We use ritual to build magical mindsets and have abilities that we can then employ on the fly. Meanwhile, even rituals that don't center the practice of spells still involve the creation of sacred space, crossing boundaries into other worlds, and shifting consciousness, which are all magical acts by practically any occult definition we could use. Witches use ritual and magic to change the world and to change themselves. So, yes, it's true that there's a lot more to Witchcraft than just working spells and conducting spooky ritual, but that initial attraction that lures so many of us isn't shallow or misguided, either. Ritual and magic are foundational, thus it makes sense that we learn to do both well.

In this chapter, we'll take a close look at the function of ritual in Witchcraft, as well as the skills and perspectives that are necessary for engaging with it effectively. We'll also consider some of what's behind the practice of magic, and what foundations we can lay to become more effective magicians.

Making Meaning

Even though this was part of what attracted me in the first place, I had been exploring Witchcraft for a long time before performing my first ritual or casting my first spell. Years, really. I was reading books and learning what I could from others, but I had to get over something of a hump before I took things any further than ambient candles, collecting magical trinkets, and tentative whispered prayers to gods I wasn't sure were real. Until very recently I would have told you that I didn't know what all that hesitation was about. I can remember the exact moment I decided to just go for it too! I was sitting outside on Halloween, finishing up with the last of the year's trick-or-treaters and just feeling the spirit of the season. Suddenly, it just sort of hit me that the night didn't have to end when the candy ran out. I could go do *Witchcraft*! And I ran inside and grabbed a notebook, sketching out a ritual based on those I'd seen in books. It was short, and performing it in my bedroom with no prior experience was more than a little awkward, but it was also heartfelt, and it laid the foundation for more to come. What had held me back for so long? It wasn't much longer before I tried my first spell. I had crossed a threshold.

Recently, though, I reread some of the very first books I ever had about Witchcraft, and I also sat down and read my journals from that time (another great reason to keep magical records). The answer was immediately obvious: I had been not just instructed but *warned* to take it slow, to study hard first, and then to be cautious about following various protocol. These books—all popular, all still in circulation among beginners today—warned of all that would happen if I messed up. From making sure the quarters were aligned properly in a magic circle, to not invoking certain deities unless I was worthy enough, to not memorizing things adequately, to doing a ritual out of a book instead of writing my own (or, conversely, having the gall to write my own instead of doing something tried and true)...there was just so much to screw up! No wonder it took me so long to work up the courage.

None of those authors or first teachers were out to scare me. They were simply sharing their own experiences and what they had found important in their own development. When we engage in something as transformative as Witchcraft, even dabbling can have consequences, but those are usually emotional and social. Left to fill in the blanks, it makes sense that many of us, especially from Christian backgrounds, would worry about offending gods, conjuring malevolent spirits, or accidentally working destructive magic. However, my own years of experience have taught me that the gods are too busy to be worried about the missteps of beginners, magic takes practice and is unlikely to explode your life the first time you try it, and malevolent spirits bent on doing us harm are largely a holdover from past religious experience and horror movies (and where they exist, like gods, they tend to be less interested in us than we ourselves are). Instead, the worst thing that can happen to us as we take our first steps into ritual practice is, well, nothing. It is infinitely more likely that you'll leave wondering if what you did worked or being disappointed later to realize it didn't. And then you'll be left to think about how you might improve, practice more in the future, and become more effective over time. And that's not a bad thing at all!

The word *ritual* gets tossed around quite a lot in different spaces, and it usually (and in the broadest possible sense) means something that we do repetitively, consistently. Sometimes used interchangeably with *routine*, ritual is something that extends beyond religious practice. Through repetition, ritual allows us to build structure into our lives and ascribe meaning where there might have been none before. It helps us mark the passage of time, draw attention to what's important, and cause tangible change in what's going on around us. Weddings, funerals, baptisms, and graduations are all familiar types of rituals, but so are football games, birthday parties, ghost stories around the campfire, and the encore after the big stadium concert. Rituals help us to tell stories about ourselves and enact those stories to make them true. They may be formal or informal, religious or not. Ritual is at the foundation of much of what we, as Witches, do.

Ritual serves many purposes, and whole books have been devoted to expounding on the theory of ritual, but for our purposes the most essential is meaning making. Ritual is a way for us to take our ideas about the nature of the world and our place in it and act them out in such a way that we make sense of our own existence. It builds order, creates a mythos, and defines our individual relationships—with ourselves and others, with whatever gods or spirits we may believe in, and with the universe as a whole. Good ritual temporarily removes us from our mundane realities—which may be chaotic, dissatisfying, exhausting, or even just boring—and creates a pocket of time when we are in control (or perhaps our gods are, depending on perspective) and can recreate the world as we see fit. Great ritual transcends that singular moment and enables us to feel those same effects out in the day to day. Ritual isn't just an escape hatch or a tool for changing the things we don't like; it's also a way to augment what's beautiful about the world. There may be an infinite variety in how people perform ritual, especially if we look across religious and cultural traditions as a whole, beyond Witchcraft, but they all seek to provide participants with a sense of purpose and meaning.

For Witches, that could mean creating the space to enact our will in the world through magic. It could also mean engaging in pageantry or sacred drama to share in stories about the gods and help us foster deeper relationships with them. For Wiccans and other Witches drawing from European esoteric traditions, the act of casting the circle and building the sacred temple between the worlds is one of world-building. As the four elements combine to create the universe, so do we invoke and combine them in its re-creation, with us as divine engineers. The specific nature of your rituals makes no matter—you could be celebrating a season, giving thanks to ancestral spirits, or casting a spell. What matters is that you find meaning in that ritual and that it fuels you to continue engaging in the world from day to day.

This is why so many of us turn to ritual in times of crisis, joy, or stress or to mark change, even those of us who identify as secular. It's not usually enough to simply bury someone; we host funerals. We mark significant relationships with weddings, the end of schooling with graduations, and births with community welcoming rituals. We also believe in the power of speech acts: public declarations that we believe bind the people who make them, as when doctors and police officers swear oaths upon joining their fields, or when those who appear in court are asked to swear on significant objects to tell the truth. Ritual transcends religion, allowing us to make meaning and create order throughout our lives. It seems to be hardwired into our humanity. But not everyone agrees that all rituals are equally meaningful (people break oaths all the time, and plenty of people don't believe in weddings or funerals). Just because something is part of established tradition doesn't mean it's going to succeed at being meaningful for everyone there.

When Witches struggle with ritual, it's often because we're having difficulty with matters related to meaning making. Newcomers frequently describe feeling silly trying to pull off their first rituals, or else worry that they're going to do something wrong. Those who've been around for a long time sometimes grow bored, lose sight of what's important, or else begin to stagnate, the meaning leeching away unnoticed. There's also just a lot of pressure within our communities and our literature to perform elaborate, regular ritual, and for a lot of us this just isn't very realistic all the time. We'll discuss solutions to this in both this chapter and the next.

Power

Like ritual, magic is a broad category that may include a variety of acts, from the casting of circles to aspecting deities to carving and burning candles. You perhaps have already been exposed to Dion Fortune's definition that magic is "the art of causing changes to take place in consciousness in accordance with will."[18] Aleister Crowley's famous assertion was that magic is "the science and art of causing change to occur in conformity with Will."[19] With these as our parameters, the bounds of magic may potentially be infinite. Anything we do might be magical. Even so, when most people think of Witchcraft, they think of spells—the use of symbolic tools and devices to direct one's intentions into reality. Sometimes spells are performed in partnership with other entities, like gods or ancestors,

---

18. Dion Fortune, "The Rationale of Magic," *London Forum* 60 (September 1934): 175–81.

19. Aleister Crowley, *Magick: Liber ABA, Book 4* (York Beach: Samuel Weiser, 1997), 127.

or with the understanding that the components of the spell, especially plants and stones, have consciousness of their own that must be invoked for assistance. The emphasis, however, tends to be on the power of the Witch themselves. Unlike many other kinds of magic, spells place primary agency on the practitioner, rather than on external powers, like gods or spirits. Thus, spellcasting transcends any one religious framework or traditional worldview. Potentially anyone can cast spells, drawing on whatever religious and cultural systems are meaningful to them.

When outsiders criticize people who pursue Witchcraft, whether for becoming Witches themselves or approaching them as clients, they often focus on their supposed need for power. Even in academic spaces, this has historically been one of the defining differences between "magic" and "religion," For Émile Durkheim, whom we met in an earlier chapter, religion and magic were inherently opposed because magicians were fundamentally self-serving, undermining communal bonds and systems, whereas religion was concerned with constructing them. Later, anthropologists like I. M. Lewis would argue that magic—and particularly magic involving bodily possession by spirits—was the provenance of the disenfranchised. Here was a way for marginalized people who would otherwise find themselves subject to the whims of others in positions of power to have some semblance of agency. The idea that magic is the tool of the outsider, the ignorant, and the powerless, whereas religion belongs to the civilized, the educated, and the elite, persisted across disciplines until relatively recently, and it survives in popular conversation still. This is at least part of the reason why a modern Witch might be ridiculed for believing that his candle spell could help him heal an illness, yet we tend to accept that praying for a sick person to recover is both reasonable and respectable. The difference lies in the location of agency. Collectively, we tend to be deeply uncomfortable with individuals who assert that they possess power outside of established social parameters and regulated systems.

This discomfort follows us into magical spaces sometimes, though, and lingers even after we become Witches. Some of the most intense debates among Witches of all kinds are over how magic should be used and where the boundaries of spellcasting should lie. Many—but certainly not all—Wiccans have answered this with the Wiccan Rede, "An it harm none, do as ye will." Other Witches find this overly limiting and maintain their own personal codes of magical conduct. To me, this is actually one of the most empowering and challenging components of the Craft. We are all responsible for our own choices and are required to draw whatever boundaries we will on our own, even where we may belong to specific traditions. We'll talk a little more about developing a personal code shortly, but for now it is worth considering your relationship with power.

For so long we've been shamed (and shamed ourselves) for seeking power. So many of us are quick to deny that the appeal of Witchcraft may lie in its emphasis on casting spells. We stigmatize the performance of spells for personal gain or frivolity. We prioritize the image of the Witch as a healer, as a wisdom keeper, or as a priest. Even the oft-cited dichotomy of "high magic" versus "low magic" posits a hierarchy, with the latter coming second. Finding love, winning money, punishing gossipers, or finding a parking spot become less noble than evolving spiritually or acquiring universal wisdom, though most people find them more pressing in the moment (if the popularity of books on the shelves and the sort of inquiries in my inbox are any indication). Curiously, we even damper our magic by insisting that it's purely about our thoughts. Intention triumphs above all else, and magic becomes just a matter of changing perspectives or reframing mundane tasks (and of course it can be, but this is not all it is). It is as though we are afraid of the power we desire to wield or, conversely, afraid that it simply isn't real.

But effective magic requires that we approach it without fear or shame. Spellcasting persists across time and peoples—transcending any one religious or cultural framework—because it works. It's perfectly natural to desire power and control over one's life and circumstances. There are a lot of different ideas floating around about how magic actually works, but this is perhaps less important than that it *does*. If you haven't already, consider picking up a few of the countless books of spells commercially available. For a beginner, it's worth simply taking the time to read as many as possible, noting patterns and similarities. Which types appeal to you and why? Try several, taking the time between them to note their effects. For more experienced practitioners, focus on the author's magical framework and ethical code. What's acceptable to them? What's not? How do they think magic works? Do you agree? What do you notice about spells that work versus spells that don't?

Above all, I encourage you to embrace the practice of spellcasting as an essential tool of the Witch. Don't dismiss it as secondary, and use it gleefully, with the understanding that you are responsible for your actions.

Serious Play

One of the reasons why Witchcraft is so tantalizing, I think, is because it speaks to something from childhood, be it our actual childhoods or the idyllic ones we wish we'd had (and all children deserve). Kids' books are full of magical tropes that influence us long after we become adults. When I read my first books on Witchcraft, magic, and polytheism, I couldn't help flashing back to my own favorites: Zilpha Keatley Snyder's *The Egypt Game*, Frances Hodgson Burnett's *A Little Princess* and *The Secret Garden*, and Roald Dahl's *Matilda*. All feature children living secret magical lives, apart from the drudgery of adulthood.

Being a Witch is a little like having a double life and access to a magical otherworld—a Terabithia or a Narnia—that only a lucky few even know exists. Doing ritual is like consciously plugging into this childish sense of wonder. But that feeling of childishness is also inhibiting for a lot of Witches, especially in the beginning. Does ritual seem difficult because you feel stupid? Does your spellcasting suffer because you doubt yourself? These are common concerns, especially for people who come to the Craft when they're older. As exciting as it might sound on paper, it's hard not to feel goofy standing alone in your bedroom casting a circle, waving a magic stick around, and reciting lots of florid poetry because you heard it can change your life and you want it to be true. I've got one of those professional cubicle jobs and a closet full of sensible shoes—believe me, I know how ridiculous my religion sounds to other people. I should get some kind of commission every time someone finds out I'm a Witch and says, "But you're smart!" or "But you look normal!" People said the same kinds of things to me in graduate school (because surely only intellectually stunted people think that they're Witches, right?).

Even if you're not lucky enough to have people calling you silly to your face, you might have a voice inside of your head picking up that slack. I know I did. We get good at discouraging ourselves and discounting our experiences, chiding ourselves for being foolish or gullible. What if someone walked in and saw? What if someone heard you through the walls? Getting over that self-consciousness can feel like a giant hurdle. There are solutions, though, and they entail taking advantage of that voice in your head calling you childish.

There's been plenty written in the fields of psychology and education about the role that play fills in the development of children. Aside from encouraging creativity, autonomy, and dexterity, it actually helps with brain development itself. Play is no less important as we age. When I worked as a teacher, my seventeen- and eighteen-year-olds also required periods of play in the classroom to retain new knowledge, to regulate their moods, and to build relationships and cognitive connections. Play, it turns out, is serious business. Adults are often discouraged from engaging in play, unless it's channeled into sanctioned sports and games. Dressing up and playing pretend becomes acceptable in theater, at Renaissance festivals, in cosplay, and in live-action role-playing (but even these things often draw derision from onlookers who think participants are questionable). But whether it's Halloween costumes or football, video games or tabletop games, we all need to play in order to be healthy and happy.

Ritual—as serious as it is—is also a form of play. It might involve costumes, special tools, the use of special names, unique rules, and skills that are equally at home on stage or film. Reciting memorized lines, altering the character of your voice, adopting a new persona, imagining new songs and poems, and plenty more besides are all strategies we use equally in pretend and in magic and ritual. The skills of Witchcraft are the skills of healthy, well-adjusted children, encouraged to play as they grow up. I believe this is one of the reasons why Witchcraft feels like "coming home" for so many of us. It's either a return to a lost childhood, or else it's the opportunity to experience the joy our childhood should have been.

If you begin to think of your magical practice as play and you accept that play is healthy and necessary at all stages of life, then much of the anxiety surrounding respectability melts away. It becomes enough just to enjoy whatever you're doing, be it dancing in your living room to celebrate May Day or wearing dramatic makeup to lead your coven in a full

moon rite. Yes, invoking gods and summoning spirits is absolutely serious work, but it's also *fun*. It's cathartic and stimulating and empowering—exactly what play is for children. Sneaking into the woods at night,
keeping secrets, waving a blade in the air, and lighting candles in the
dark is *fun*, no matter how many exclusive initiations you've had or how
old you get. Ask any ten-year-old. Allowing your Craft to be fun—to consciously be a form of play—will build your confidence, which in turn will
make it more effective.[20]

Baneful Magic, Cursing, and You

When I first began practicing Witchcraft back in the late nineties, there
was an almost phobic attitude about any sort of manipulative or baneful magic. Most of the books available stressed immediately and repetitively that Witches never worked negative magic, nor did they work with
demons, believe in any kind of devil, or conduct themselves in ways that
could potentially do harm to others. The Wiccan Rede dominated, sometimes even among Witches who themselves weren't quick to identify
their Craft specifically as Wicca. Even the Witches portrayed in popular
media—as in the show *Charmed*—were unable to work magic for personal
gain. Witches were benign stewards of nature, gentle healers, and misunderstood keepers of an ancient wisdom, if you accepted the image pro-
moted by Pagan media of the day.

Looking back, many will assert that all of this was the result of the
disproportionate attention placed on Wiccan Witchcraft at the expense
of other traditions, but while it's certainly true that Wicca dominated,
the full picture is somewhat more complicated. The nineties came on the
heels of a period in American history characterized by an intense fear of
anything even perceived to be in any way tied to the occult, Witchcraft,
Satanism, or the supernatural. Nicknamed the Satanic Panic, fueled by

---

20. And if anyone really does hear you through the walls or walks in on you unannounced,
    you can tell them you're practicing for community theater or making your own movie
    to post online. As an additional tip, it's much easier to get away with performing
    ritual outside in public spaces if you first place a camera on a tripod and aim it at
    yourself (even in an "off" position). Passersby will assume you're acting as part of a
    project and you can bypass the discomfort of potentially having to defend your
    unusual religious proclivities.

a rash of accusations of ritual child abuse against a number of daycare employees as well as by the rise of a particular kind of fundamentalist Christianity, the eighties and nineties were a potentially dangerous time to be open about being a practicing Witch. A number of innocent people went to jail and remained there for *years*. Then, in April of 1999, the shooting in Littleton, Colorado, at Columbine High School perpetrated by two trench coat–clad students reputed to have connections to the occult turned Goth and punk teenagers into easy scapegoats. Schools all over the country—including my own—began to police students inclined toward dark clothing, occult jewelry, and anything else deemed "alternative." It's little wonder that Witches of the day were so vocal about being harmless, whether or not it was strictly true. It wasn't just Wiccans who were anxiously plastering "harm none" on every website and insisting that Witchcraft was a life-affirming religion, deserving of federal protection like any other. Persecution as a Witch was not the abstraction that it is for most of us today.

It's a little strange, having grown up during the tail end of the Satanic Panic, to now be practicing in an age when baneful magic is so de rigueur. Lots of people are quick to hex and curse, to work manipulative spells, and to explore traditions and techniques that would have been taboo only a decade ago. On the one hand, it's exciting, because these have always been an important component of historical Witchcraft as well as some of the earliest contemporary traditions. It feels like we're reclaiming something that should never have been taken from us or forgotten. On the other hand, it lends itself to abuse by the cavalier. We plant toxic herbs in our homes because they make us feel hardcore and provide great fodder for social media, but they can kill the careless nonetheless. We can use magic to punish abusers and curtail wrongdoers, but who needs punishing and curtailing may be less clear than we choose to believe. Our enemies have as much access to magic as we do, after all.

I'm not here to tell anyone not to explore baneful magic, and I'm certainly not of the mindset that cursing is never justified. There's a pile of skeletons in my closet too, and I'm not sorry about it. However, if magic is real—and I believe it is—then so are its consequences. If you choose to use it as a weapon, then have the respect to treat it with the *care* of a weapon.

Whether you're new to the Craft or an experienced practitioner, it's important to consciously develop a personal code of ethics. When is magic appropriate and justified? Are there ever circumstances when it's not? How do you feel about using magic for personal gain? Many Witches won't, for a variety of reasons. What about working beneficial magic but without the consent of your target? How is it that you know what's best for someone else? How will you be confident that your decisions are sound?

If you haven't already, answer these questions for yourself now, before you're actually backed into a corner where you potentially have to make a difficult choice on the spot. If you work with gods or spirits, consult them. Ask other Witches. Be willing to listen to conflicting perspectives, make well-reasoned choices, and then have the integrity to stand by them when it might be unpopular to do so.

Fireworks and Birdsong

Sometimes the effects of a spell or a ritual are instantaneous. When the mood is just right, the energy flows, and things go off without a hitch, it's like a lightning strike. You just *know* it's working. The buzz of a great ritual can last for days afterward. A well-crafted and well-timed spell, packed with a clear intention and precise boundaries can begin to work immediately and obviously. And wouldn't it be great if that's how it went every time?

Magic—whether we're talking about spells or marking the phases of the moon through ritual—is truly incredible. I'm not exaggerating in the least when I say it's changed my life, but it hasn't been the fireworks show that so many people expect when they first begin exploring Witchcraft. In fact, it's very rarely anything close. One of the reasons why many struggle with magic and ritual is because they begin with unreasonable expectations of what it should look like. Even those of us who've relinquished most of the magical thinking of childhood find it rekindled at a soul level when we first learn that Witches are real and there is power and wonder out there to be freely harnessed. We know that what we're doing isn't supernatural. We can't start fires with our minds or levitate. . .but deep down I don't think most of us ever really stop thinking it *might* be possible. We understand that when we encounter a spirit, it will surely be in a visionary state and not literally manifested in the flesh before us. Our shapeshifting is either astral or metaphorical, and not physical. We create paths of least resistance for magic to flow; we don't defy natural laws. But the children still within our psyches haven't relinquished their hope, and as adults, it is still difficult to learn that magic is almost never the obvious, undeniable spectacle we wish it were.

One of the most profound things about practicing magical ritual is that it creates a space where there is possibility. We are never powerless as Witches. We can step into sacred space at will. In our rituals, when wielding our tools—whether spell accoutrements or the mind alone—we are in control. Over time that sense of control will inevitably alter your relationship with the world outside your magical spaces. You may find that you become more confident, more directed, or more self-contained. Those things alone will make your magic more successful, but before you even arrive here, know that the key to profound results and the thing you should strive for is an increased sensitivity to your surroundings. There may be no fireworks to alert you when a spell is working, but a sharp awareness and appreciation for the world will do the same.

My friend Rhi likes to point to Robert Frost's poem "Never Again Would Birds' Song Be the Same," in which an unidentified narrator reflects on the effect that the voice of Eve—perhaps the woman he loves, perhaps the biblical Eve, perhaps a metaphor for life itself—has on the birds singing in the wood. She speaks and laughs, and the birds add her song to theirs. Eve's voice crosses with those of the birds, such that even after she's gone her song persists, fundamentally altering how everyone else hears birdsong though they may not be conscious of it. "Never again would birds' song be the same," Frost writes, "And to do that to birds was why she came."[21] Eve raising her voice in the garden changes the fabric woven by the creatures around her. The narrator can hear her in the music of the birds and knows that the effects will be there even after she is gone. The key here is that in order to understand the power of Eve's

---

21. Robert Frost, *A Witness Tree* (New York: Henry Holt and Company, 1942), 24.

presence, one has to have stopped to listen to the birds, before and after she herself passed through the wood.

This, Rhi will tell you, is how magic works. It absolutely changes the world, even to the point where it seems supernatural, but that doesn't mean those effects will be obvious and undeniable. Birdsong might seem meaningless, and often goes completely unheard, even where it permeates the landscape, but if you train yourself to listen for it and to see the beauty inherent there, nothing could be more extraordinary.

It's normal to experience doubt as a Witch. Sometimes I think insecurity leads people to exaggerate their experiences when they share them with other Witches and magicians. This in turn alters the expectations of those listening, especially if they're beginners who are desperate for earthshaking transformation. No one wants to be the person who has never seen fireworks, especially when our inner, younger selves long for them. But magic is usually much more subtle than that. You learn to appreciate synchronicity and come to believe that perhaps nothing is coincidence. You find meaning in what you hear and see, where previously things went ignored. No longer does the song on the radio feel like chance. You notice patterns—repeating numbers and shapes or the mention of someone you haven't thought about in years and have been meaning to call.

Those moments when all your hairs stand on end and you swear you've just encountered something definitely otherworldly will also happen, but you won't require them with every lit candle and whispered chant. Growing as a magician means that the song of birds is extraordinary by itself, and that it will never be the same once you've heard what lies underneath.

When It Doesn't Come Naturally

There are a potentially infinite number of ways to engage in ritual. Because so many of us are exposed to Witchcraft through the same channels—Wicca-flavored introductory texts, public Pagan circles, and popular Witchy media—we tend to settle into one or two formats and then beat them to death. That might be okay. When you're practicing something that is truly effective and fuels you on a deep level, then repetition over time can build and deepen that power. That's the beauty of tradition. But what if those most-typical ritual styles and techniques just don't do it for you?

For years, I thought that there was something wrong with me—that I was magically deficient or otherwise incapable of being an effective Witch. I would go to open rituals out in my local community, and I would follow instructions in books, and they would, well...leave me sort of cold. I loved meeting other Witches and exploring this new world full of possibilities, but over and over again I'd find myself standing in circles with enrapt, intense people, breathing heavily, eyes closed and swaying, and I would feel nothing. What made it worse was mingling afterward and hearing people describe their experiences in such detail: "I could see the Goddess standing with us in circle," or "The energy was really power-ful tonight," or "I could feel the magic moving through me." Was I just insensitive? A brick wall where magic was concerned?

In retrospect, I'm kind of amazed at myself for sticking it out as long as I did. A longtime fan of *Buffy the Vampire Slayer*, I started to think of myself as the Xander of the community—the character with no special powers, no supernatural talents, who contributed to the team's evil-fighting antics through mundane means. Others brought the woo; I brought the snacks or helped secure the space. Important jobs, to be sure, but what a bleak out-look! Who wants to discover magic is real only to be relegated to the role of human sidekick?

It took going to my first festival and then practicing with an intimate traditional coven to experience something more akin to what I'd heard was possible. The festival provided opportunities for me to see non-Wiccan ritual for the first time (what does it look like when there isn't a quartered circle and a paired priestess and priest?). The coven taught me that things are possible in small spaces among close friends that don't translate to big public gatherings. I learned, for example, that sound is a huge ritual trigger for me. Singing, chanting, and drumming really enhance my magic and my focus, which makes sense since I'm a musi-cian. The downside is that I can be distracted by jarring sounds: slightly off-beat drumming (i.e., all open drum circles), dissonant singing, or even background music that feels out of place to me. In a small setting where I'm leading, I can use this knowledge about myself to enhance things. In a public space, I had to learn to work around others. But as a new Witch, none of this was obvious to me. All I knew was that I struggled while everyone else seemed to be having life-changing experiences.

Over time and with practice, I learned more techniques that were effective for me. It's really not unlike food: just because everyone around you loves pizza, that doesn't mean you have to. It certainly doesn't mean there's anything wrong with you if you'd rather eat something else. Pizza might even make you sick, or you might prefer to save it for certain occasions. Rituals with big groups of people standing in a circle while someone in the center performs a Wiccan-style invocation is like pizza. It works for many, but there are other options out there. Take the time to explore by reading widely, participating in different kinds of groups, and getting creative in your own ritual writing. As a solitary Witch, especially, there isn't anyone there to criticize you. So try things, be open to failure, and be honest with yourself if something just isn't doing it for you.

There's also a popular Craft aphorism that says coming to Witchcraft is like coming home. We often talk about our practices in terms of feeling "natural" or like discovering our "true selves." More than once I've heard practitioners say that if Witchcraft doesn't come easily, students should take that as an indication that the Craft may not be for them.

That's hogwash.

Can you imagine what a parent would say if I told them that we should take their child's struggle to read as indication that reading just wasn't for them? In a just system, I would be excused from the classroom.

There are things about Witchcraft that feel easy and natural, but effective ritual and magic are skill sets, and they come easier to some than to others. There are whole systems designed to train initiates over the course of years to communicate with a specific deity, to work a particular rite, or to develop some seemingly supernatural power. Not being able to pull something off right away or in certain circumstances doesn't make you unsuited for Witchcraft. It makes you pretty much like the rest of us: good at some things and less so at others, with unique talents and proclivities, and lots of room for improvement all around. Twenty years of hanging out with other Witches has also shown me that an awful lot of us exaggerate our abilities and experiences to cover up feelings of inadequacy. No one wants to be the one to say, "I didn't feel anything" or "I've never been successful at that." No longer do I believe that every person standing in the ritual space with their eyes closed, looking intense and breathing dramatically is every time having some transformative experience. Some are, yes, but most are doing what we're all doing: trying. And that's not nothing.

It's okay to struggle with any given technique (or to throw it away if it doesn't work for you), and it's okay to say, "Nah, I didn't really get anything out of that." Take note of your experiences over time, try to discern patterns, and celebrate the progress you make. Good ritual takes practice, just like anything else worth doing.

• EXERCISE •
Performing Meaning

The key to good ritual and effective magic is *regularity*. You don't have to engage in them every day (though it's helpful to imagine your everyday activities as magical), but it is important that whatever you do is consistent and focused. Being in magical space, feeling the flow of energy, encountering entities like deities and spirits, working magic, and building the kind of meaning that you can take out of ritual and bring back to your daily life all require the building of particular skills and perspectives. And that takes exposure, practice, experimentation, and development! The following exercises are designed to get you into ritual space and working magic that fuels you, wherever you happen to be in your own Craft practice.

Air

In my years of working with beginners, I've found over and over again that the biggest holdup for newcomers to Witchcraft is taking the leap from reading about ritual to getting up and doing it. In my own early journals, I repeatedly describe feelings of self-consciousness, worry about doing something wrong, and practically obsess over whether or not Witchcraft is real or I'm really a Witch (the general consensus seemed to be that it was real, but I was probably a fraud). I hear similar concerns from students today, and I see it over and over again in communities, both online and off. Even those of us who feel Witchcraft deep in our bones often hesitate to do the work of the Witch, almost always because we lack confidence. "Oh, I'm just going to read as much as I can first and take it slow," we tell ourselves, or, "I want to find a teacher first and become an initiate so I know I'm doing it right." Or my personal favorite, "I get just as much out of the Craft just reading about it—I visualize and journal and pray. I don't need to do ritual, because I can just imagine it really clearly."

The longer you wait, the more difficult it gets to take the plunge, just like standing on the edge of cold water right before you jump in. Whatever excuse you're using, put it down. I don't care if this is the first book you've ever picked up on the subject. I don't care if the full moon isn't for weeks, we're nowhere near a sabbat, and you've got no fancy tools. I especially don't care if someone told you the world would explode if you did it wrong. Go *do* something. It can be something simple, like casting a circle and then taking it back down. It can be you lighting a candle and reciting an invocation to a deity that appeals to you. Go choose a spell out of your favorite spellbook and do it. Flip back to the chapter on sacred space and cleanse your bedroom. Take something directly out of a book because it looks cool, or try your hand at writing something original. Right now, it matters a lot more that you get over the initial fear of "What if I do it wrong?" and just take a stab at it. There are lots of horror stories floating around about what can happen to you if you mess up, but most of these are little more than urban legend, circulated by people trying to freak you out. You'll probably feel silly and awkward. Embrace it! Laugh! Call a magical friend up afterward and tell them how goofy you felt, so they can then tell you about their goofy first rituals (because they have a story or two, I guarantee it). On the other hand, you might have an amazing experience and leave feeling excited to learn more and do even better the next time.

Seriously, why are you still reading? Go!

Fire

Lots of Witches struggle sometimes with working effective spells, especially when time is limited and stress is high. One way to boost the effectiveness of a working, or to evaluate one that you're considering performing, is to turn to a technique popular in corporate spaces: SMART goals. I first learned about the SMART framework as an athlete, learning to work through training programs to improve my time and distance as a runner. Later, I encountered them again as a project manager in an office, managing a team and working with clients. It turns out that this is a helpful way to approach spellcasting too!

SMART is a mnemonic device that stands for specific, measurable, achievable, relevant, and time-bound. Each of these is a criterion that, when in place, makes results more easily obtainable, whether we're talking about a fitness goal, a project at work, or a spell. Using the SMART strategy, we not only ensure that our intentions are crystal clear, but we also put in any necessary limitations and determine how we're going to measure effectiveness and in what time frame. It might look something like this:

Let's say I dream of running an online business, perhaps selling tarot card readings or original pieces of artwork. I have a straight job in an office to make ends meet, but it's my dream to be able to quit and operate my own business full time. I decide that I'm going to do a spell to help me get there (on top of all the usual legwork, because of course we need to be covering our mundane bases too). I could just charge a candle for business success, write an incantation, and then burn it while the moon is waxing (and maybe throw in some planetary timing, while we're at it), but taking the extra effort to apply SMART to my spell could give me an extra boost here, and with minimal effort.

First, I need to get specific (there's that first letter). What exactly do I define as "business success"? I mean, my goal is to not have to work in an office, but what's it going to take to get there? How much money do I need to bring in every month? Do that math. If I'm just starting out, "business success" could be making one sale in the first few days, but is that really going to satisfy me? If I'm careless and instead focus on not being in an office, I could just as easily find myself getting laid off, rather than finding success in what I actually dream of doing. So be specific! If "business success" means "I make $3,000 every month" or "I make 25 sales every week," then that's what you need to specify.

This covers our second letter, *M*, too. Sometimes it's helpful to create spells that are open-ended, but it gets old working with abstractions and wondering if your magic is really working, or if you're just believing in it to keep yourself from feeling like it was a wash. I don't think we should need to squint quite so hard and move the goalposts in order to declare our magic successful. It feels good to be able to objectively say, "Yes, this worked." What's more, it's perfectly possible. How will you measure if your spell was a success? In this example, I could choose a specific number ($3,000 per month, 25 sales per week, or whatever else I came up with). You might also choose something like "I can pay all my utility bills with my earnings," or something else that's a little more open-ended but still measurable. The end result is a simple yes or no to the question "Did this spell work?"

The next letter is key. The outcome of your spell needs to actually be achievable. If I only opened my online business yesterday and have no website and no client base, it would be unreasonable to expect that it would make me a millionaire overnight. Consider what mundane circumstances are already in place, consider what is reasonable, and then (because we are Witches, after all), push it a little further than what you would expect to achieve without the use of magic.

Next, I need to make sure my spell lines up with the actual outcome I want. In other words, I need to ensure that it's relevant. I'm trying to start an online business and I'm hoping that my side hustle takes off, but I need to ask myself what my actual goal is. Do I want to be a successful tarot reader, or do I just not want to work a nine-to-five office job anymore? Do I want to sell my art, or do I really just want the time and money to be allowed to create art unhindered? Those are all different goals, and they don't necessarily line up. Ask yourself why you're doing the spell, and what it is you *really* want. Do the spell for the end itself, not for the means to that end.

Finally, it's helpful to place a time frame on any spell that you work. This keeps things from working too late, too long, or intermittently. If I decide to work my spell to succeed in my online business, and I decide that my criterion for success is going to be earning $3,000, I need to put that in the context of time. A tarot reader who makes $3,000 in one week is quite wealthy, and certainly a success by most standards, but one who makes $3,000 over the course of their entire career is far from it. Put a timeframe in place! Even on things like protection spells, spells for good health, and other workings that would ideally be indefinite. If you add in limitations concerning time, you can be more thorough in your coverage and also get into the habit of refreshing and recharging workings that actually require more effort than most people want to put into them.

Talking about SMART goals can feel a little corporate in magical spaces, but this is actually a really helpful system for developing laser focus in magic. It will also help you modify spells that you encounter in books and online so that they suit your needs more directly.

Water

Not every Witch celebrates the eight sabbats, which really came to exist in their current form thanks to the influence of Wicca specifically. However, most of us mark seasonal change of some kind or another, whether that means working with the sabbats or celebrating other holy days rooted in folklore or specific regional or ethnic tradition. Annual cycles are important to Witches, and I bet you've got a favorite holiday or two. But a lot of our traditions have been imported, exported, modified in contemporary times, and otherwise removed from their original contexts, which can make it difficult to connect with them on a deep level. A lot of our common festivals are agricultural, for example, and have perhaps lost some of their meaning since overwhelmingly we aren't farmers, don't raise animals, and maybe don't ever set foot in wild natural spaces. I mean, the very first time someone explained the sabbat of Imbolc to me, they launched into a speech about the lactation of sheep. What the hell did that have to do with me, living in a suburb outside a major city?

There have been some great works written recently about reframing the Wiccan Wheel of the Year for our real lives, rather than for some idealized agrarian lifestyle that we don't actually live. In many styles of Traditional Witchcraft, practitioners emphasize getting outside and observing the cycles of the plants and animals that actually live around you, rather than relying on stories about (usually Western European) spaces that have no bearing on the land actually under your feet. Whether you live on a farm or in a tiny apartment in a gargantuan city, you are part of an annual cycle, shifting from season to season (however many seasons you have), marked with animal migrations, cultural happenings, events in your body, and potentially myriad other factors.

For this exercise, you're going to add a holy day of your choosing to your ritual calendar. Rather than rewrite those that you already celebrate (which you should also try, by the way), design an entirely new one. Consider your year. What special days do you celebrate apart from those established within whatever tradition of Witchcraft you practice? Are there any that could benefit from formal ritual celebration? You could choose something prominent and obvious, like a loved one's birthday, or a feast day relevant to a favorite deity. You could choose a civil holiday and make it magical. But you could also use this as an opportunity to explore natural cycles that usually go completely unmarked and unnoticed. I like to celebrate when the wisteria finally starts blooming here in North Carolina, because that's when it really feels like spring to me. Perhaps design a ritual to welcome back or say goodbye to your favorite migratory bird. Do you live somewhere that experiences hurricane season? What if you consciously harnessed that?

Get creative. Choose something that has significance for you year after year, but which you may have never formally acknowledged. Then write a ritual, perhaps in the style of whatever tradition you already follow. Over time, you might choose to continue with this practice, or to add to it. Who knows—in a few years, you might have an entirely new Wheel of the Year, perfectly in tune with your lived experience.

Earth

A funny thing starts to happen to you when you spend years and years working a particular tradition or system of Witchcraft: you sort of start to forget that you ever did anything else in the past or that other things are even possible (let alone effective). When we become entrenched in one way of doing things, especially over the course of a decade or two, sometimes our flexibility and creativity can suffer a little. Recently, I was startled to go through one of my very first magical journals and to discover that I used to use entirely different elemental associations. I had just finished explaining to someone why it was that we tied the athame to Air and the east, and that I couldn't imagine doing anything different, and here I was, proving myself wrong from the past.

In another magical venture, I began studying within a different tradition, purely (or so I thought) for the sake of broadening my experience and learning new techniques that might deepen the work I was already doing. This was effective, but it required that I set aside some of the things that I'd begun to think of as foundational—even required. It was quite a challenge, and very gratifying, to find that I had the power to work effective ritual and magic in other contexts and that this only made me stronger within my home tradition.

For this exercise, I ask you to consider those things that are foundational or core to your own Craft. Not its basic theology, perhaps, but its ritual structure. Does your tradition require a particular altar setup? A quartered circle with the elements in particular directions? Do you adhere to specific gender roles within your coven? Does the same person always invoke the gods? Whatever it is, choose something that feels essential to your ritual work. Then throw it away.

Don't panic—this isn't permanent. You're doing magical science here. Allow yourself to be shaken up. Get uncomfortable. Get *really* uncomfortable. Swap your quarter associations. If your ritual calls for a priest and priestess, try it with one person. Or three. Or two of the same gender. Don't cast a circle. Remove all the sexual metaphors from your liturgy (can you still pull off Beltane?). Invoke angels. Invoke nothing but yourself. Whatever.

Allow yourself to sit with this process. Work it for an appreciable period of time, depending on the change you're making. This is about building your chops as a ritualist, not disrespecting any previous training you've had. Can you work in an unfamiliar environment? Is your Witchcraft strong enough to pull off in circumstances that don't match up to your ideal?

Chapter 5
Personal Practice

The alarm goes off at 5:00, in the wee hours of the morning. The sun won't rise for another hour. I hit snooze and lie there in the dark, already regretting my choices. I'm so tired, and I'm dreading the coming workday, which is pretty much the state of my life these days. I've been a classroom teacher for a couple of years at this point, and I'm still not used to the routine. I have to be at my post by 6:30, and the first bell rings at 7:15. I can squeak in a shower if I rush, and I recently put a coffee pot in my classroom so I don't lose time making coffee at home. Teaching is not compatible with leisurely morning routines, that's for sure! If you want more time, the cost is sleep. But by the end of the school day, I'm completely wiped out, so if I'm doing this, I need to get up and do it now. It's a new day—the first day of my new, perfect, magical daily practice.

I drag myself out of bed and sit before my altar. I light a candle, close my eyes, and try to focus on my breathing, willing myself into a meditative state. Maybe I should start practicing yoga or something. I've written a morning devotional to my gods—I like the idea of starting my day with this. Maybe if I wake up a bit earlier I could start a morning journaling practice too. I could make coffee and maybe read from one of my Witchcraft books in the growing pile on my nightstand. I could do evening devotionals too. Sure, I'm exhausted by the afternoon, but I'd get used to it. Right? I just read something about how important daily ritual is for maintaining a connection to the divine and staying centered as a Witch.

If it were important to me, I'd just do it, right? Hey, why is my mind wandering like this? I'm supposed to be meditating!

Does any of this sound familiar? We've all probably heard at this point how important a daily practice is. There's a lot of advice out there too for how to build one, how to maintain one, how to improve the one you've already got. Half of that advice, it seems, requires waking up early or staying up later, which is no easy feat if your job *already* has you up in the wee hours or working night shift. A lot of the advice we're given is solid, but a lot of it requires that you overhaul your life right out of the gate, and that all but ensures failure. In my own quest to build a meaningful personal practice, I've made a lot of mistakes. In this chapter, I'll share some of those with you so you can avoid them yourself. We'll also discuss why it's worth bothering with any of this at all and how to create something sustainable that truly serves you in the long term.

What It Means to Practice

Witchcraft, as we've established at many points already, is a *craft*. A thing that you *do*. Even if you see your own Witchcraft as a completely religious perspective (or a spiritual perspective, if you prefer) completely independent of things like ritual and spellcraft, belief implies action. At some point you may have learned that there's a distinction between orthodoxy and orthopraxy—right belief and right practice, respectively—and heard the insistence that Witchcraft tends to be orthopraxic. That's true, but it's also an overly simplistic distinction. Both are at work in the many traditions of the Craft. Even if your focus up to this point has been exploring your beliefs or stretching how you think about the gods, magic, or the world itself, it's likely that those things are showing up in how you interact with others, how you treat yourself, and in the choices you make. A personal practice is made up of all those things that you do that consciously draw your attention to your beliefs—pushing them, expanding them, and deepening them. Practice is what makes us better and takes us farther.

All those people out there stressing about how critical a personal practice is are right. This is your key for developing spiritually, for accruing magical power, for deepening any otherworldly or divine relationships you might have (or want to have), and for expanding your experience and effectiveness as a Witch. It doesn't matter what sort of Witch you are—the best thing you can do as you take your next steps is to develop your personal practice. This is equally true whether you're a solitary practitioner or a member of a group.

In Witchcraft, a personal practice might include a wide variety of actions. We tend to imagine something that entails a lot of ritual and spellcrafting, meditation and divination, but this is all only one way to approach building a practice. Yours may look different and include different things that don't seem very Witchy or magical at all to onlookers. A personal practice might include physical exercise, journaling, reading selected texts, or making art. These things by themselves aren't in and of themselves Witchcraft, but for an individual Witch who finds meaning in them, they could strengthen and feed their magical life. As a writer, for example, I rely on journaling and reading as important components of my practice of the Craft. Journaling my thoughts and experiences from day to day helps me process, clears my head, and illuminates patterns that point me toward my divine Will. Then, when I enter ritual space, I have a better sense of purpose and focus. I am able to be more discerning in my interactions in magical spaces, and my intentions are much clearer, which in turn makes my magical workings infinitely more effective. Writing is also how I connect with and serve the gods I worship. I ritualize the process by designating specific times to write, anointing and consecrating notebooks and some of my pens and ink, and augmenting my writing space with consecrated candles and incense. In this way, I take something potentially very mundane—keeping a journal—and turn it into something that fuels my Witchcraft. I know other Witches who do similar things with other mundane activities. My friend and fellow Witch author Casey Giovinco practices yoga and weightlifting to connect to his sacred, magical sense of self. My covenmate Wren is a falconer, and she uses her time working with her hawk companion to understand the gods she serves. These things alone are not Witchcraft—every dude powerlifting at the gym isn't invoking the Mighty Ones. But, hey. He could be! And you could be too, if powerlifting were your thing. If not that, perhaps something that more immediately speaks to you.

Ritual, magic, and devotional work are all important in a personal practice, but it is helpful to think holistically about your Witchcraft. What other hobbies, interests, and proclivities do you have that could be harnessed to magical ends? When you move through your day-to-day life, are you thinking and behaving like a Witch?

Why Is Practice Difficult?

I opened this chapter with a small window into a time in my life when I was really struggling with my work as a Witch. I was leading a coven and active in a number of Witchcraft communities, but I was deeply unsatisfied with my life, and it was showing up in my Craft. I knew that I needed to be working on myself and focusing on reinforcing a personal practice—regular ritual, open conversations with the gods and spirits in my life, active study, staying conscious of lunar and seasonal cycles—but I just kept dropping the thread each time. A lot of the mistakes I made are right there in that very first paragraph. Did you spot any right away? If you didn't, no worries. These are some of the most common mistakes Witches of all levels make when they're either building or revamping their magical lives.

1. Being Unrealistic about What You Will Do

The surefire way to fail at something is by taking on too much at the outset and setting the bar for yourself too high. But wait, you say. Isn't it important to have high standards for yourself? Yes, but only to a point. It's much more effective to tackle larger tasks by first breaking them into smaller tasks. If you've never been free diving before and you suddenly decide to give it a go, it would be unrealistic to stroll down to the neighborhood pool and expect to be able to hold your breath for five minutes the very first time you jump in. Nobody decides they're going to give distance running a go and then signs up for a marathon later that afternoon. So why do we think we're going to be able to meditate for half an hour in perfect stillness when we haven't yet mastered five minutes? Why do we decide we're going to go from nothing to performing devotional rituals twice a day and working elaborate spells every time the moon does something cool? And then why do we feel discouraged when gods don't talk directly to us immediately and our first spells don't work, even though occult adepts spend their whole lives developing their techniques? I decided that I was going to overhaul my personal practice and then set a bunch of unrealistic expectations for myself. When I didn't succeed right away, I got discouraged and stopped even trying.

2. Adding Too Much Too Soon

This often goes hand in hand with being unrealistic. I hadn't even mastered getting up early on a routine basis to light a candle in quiet contemplation, but there I was making plans to throw in journaling, reading, meditation, and invocation. You might already have an image in your head of what the ideal Witchcraft practice looks like, but if you try to overhaul everything all at once to get there, you're going to become overwhelmed and frustrate yourself into failure. Building a life in the Craft is a long game. Not only should you not do everything at once, you actually just can't. Sorry to be the one to tell you. In my example, I would've been better off focusing on one change at a time, introducing new elements to my budding routine gradually.

3. Not Respecting Your Needs and Limits

When you're setting new goals for yourself and building a new routine, you have to keep *yourself* in mind, not some idealized Witch who doesn't really exist. That means taking your physical needs and limitations into account, working with your schedule, acknowledging your other obligations, and taking advantage of your strengths and interests. I wasn't going to instantly transform into someone who loves being awake at five in the morning and is still totally energized at the end of a dreary workday, so why was I trying to force myself? I would've been more successful if I'd come up with a devotional practice I could do around lunchtime, when I *was* awake and fully energized. Know yourself, know your patterns, and work with them instead of pretending you're someone you're not.

4. Going In with the Wrong Attitude

Do you get the sense that rolling out of bed that morning felt like a chore to me? Because it definitely did. On top of that, I was totally focused on what I *should* be doing, where I wasn't measuring up, and what was *wrong* with me as a Witch. There wasn't any joy in the plan I'd concocted. Witchcraft is work, as we've discussed several times already. You'll face difficulty as a Witch, from deep inner exploration to cognitive dissonance, late nights, lots of reading, and probably some social disruption too. But this isn't a path of punishment or asceticism. Suffering is not a sign that you're succeeding, nor is it a virtue. So look for what fuels you, what sounds fun, what motivates you, and makes you feel good about yourself too. You shouldn't dread your personal practice, and if you are, take that as an indication to change it. When other Witches say that Witchcraft is work, they mean it takes care and effort, not that it's laborious and requires anguish.

There's a lot of talk out there about how critical it is to maintain a personal practice and the ten thousand potential things that could entail, and yet for many of us—from beginners to experienced Witches—a regular practice eludes us. If you find yourself struggling, consider if you're making any of these mistakes. Sometimes small adjustments are all that's needed to transform a lackluster level of engagement into something truly powerful and fulfilling.

Thinking Like a Witch

Have you noticed that I've been using the phrases *personal practice* and *regular practice*, and not stressing *daily practice*? Yeah, I'm doing that on purpose. Lots of books and teachers stress that Witchcraft is a lived tradition, and not just something you slip on at sabbats or when it's safe and convenient to do so. Being a Witch means living the Craft day in and day out, allowing it to root in your bones. That's all true enough. Even in the throes of deep depression, or when life just gets so chaotic I don't even feel like I can breathe, my Craft is so deeply ingrained that I'm not sure I could completely excise it even if I wanted to. But that's not because I'm holding rituals every day and constantly casting spells. The idea that Witchcraft is purely a craft and not about how you think—that it's entirely about orthopraxy—simply isn't true, convenient as that dichotomy may be. How you think, what you believe, and the actions you take because of that are all intertwined.

If you only pay attention to and give yourself credit for overt acts of magic or worship, you're selling yourself short. You're also not laying as strong of a foundation as you could, especially as you either build a practice for the first time or overhaul the one you already have. Action without feeling is meaningless—if you don't have strong beliefs surrounding what you do, then it will be easier to give up or be waylaid when things start getting inconvenient or difficult. One of the reasons why converts from other religions—as so many of us come from Christian backgrounds—*struggle* with religious guilt is because belief matters so deeply. One does not simply walk straight out of one paradigm and into another one. Conversion is a process, one that is potentially accompanied by trauma. It's not enough to just pick up a different set of ritual practices and some new jargon.

So while it's good to focus on what you're physically doing as you build your practice, don't stress about things on the daily level, especially if this is a new process for you. It's much more important that whatever you're doing is *regular*. That doesn't have to mean daily. Can you commit to something weekly? On every full and new moon? Every sabbat or other holy day in the tradition you're pursuing? We'll take a look at what kinds of things you might actually do in the next section and in the exercises at the end of this chapter, but start thinking now about what kinds of parameters you may want to start with. In the rest of your time, you'll be exploring how you think, pushing the boundaries of what you believe, and developing the *mind* of a Witch.

Adam Sartwell, one of the founders of the Temple of Witchcraft, is prone to asking, "Are you thinking like a Witch?" A simple enough question, but one worth posing regularly. Witches really do think differently, and this is something that we often have to cultivate actively. In many occult arts, our first ventures pertain to harnessing our minds, and the Craft is no different.

First, there is the fundamental belief that we have power and can influence the things that happen to us. This is the foundation of magic. As a Witch, you are never completely at the mercy of circumstance, so long as your mind is functioning. One of our perpetual goals is self-mastery. Can you maintain control and composure? Can you redirect your thoughts at will? Can you reframe whatever situation you're in and see solutions, alternative pathways, and hidden opportunities where others might only see conflict and difficulty? When you practice these skills, you're laying the foundation for Witchcraft, long before you step into a ritual space.

Next, there is the power of observation. This is a mental skill that cannot be understated. Online and at Witchcraft gatherings it's trendy to harp on empathy, but observation is much easier to cultivate and provides much of the same information. When you shut up and pay attention to all the sensory details you receive moving around in the world, it's infinitely easier to react to the circumstances that come your way, to evaluate the intentions and motivations of others, to decipher patterns and meaning in happenings that seem random, and to find inspiration and beauty in your environment. The Craft often works in subtleties. If you don't train yourself to truly *see* what's going on around you, you'll miss much of what is profound about being a Witch. Go out into unfamiliar spaces and practice often. What do you see, hear, smell? What can you know about the people around you just by observing them over time? Observation is something you can develop constantly, and this will serve you later in any other magical endeavor you may pursue.

Finally, there is the way routine settles in your psyche and in your body. You don't necessarily have to practice a lot of magic or ritual, but what you do over time will stick with you, building new habits and altering your expectations, your values, and the choices you make unconsciously. Over time, you'll develop a sense for the natural cycles around you, for what's happening in your own body, and for shifts in realms beyond this one. You won't need to hold elaborate rituals or go out of your way to be conscious of these things (though you'll probably want to anyway). They'll just be part of who you are.

So are you thinking like a Witch?

It's not enough just to *do* things—rituals, spells, meditation, reciting devotionals, or whatever. There needs to be something behind your actions. Purpose, intention, and perspective are less visible and sometimes get overlooked in all our talk of orthopraxy and "craft." Your practice of Witchcraft is as much about your mind, even though we tend to focus elsewhere.

What Are We Actually Doing?

Most types of Witchcraft rely on the same handful of techniques as building blocks for practice. If you've read other Witchcraft books or worked with any kind of teacher, you're sure to have been exposed to most of these at some point. Maybe you've even been struggling for a while with one or two.

Meditation

There are many kinds of meditation with slightly different functions, and it's worth trying several. Perhaps most common is mindfulness meditation, in which one allows one's thoughts to pass through, without attachment or judgment, ultimately allowing space to clear the mind of thoughts altogether. This is excellent for creating stillness, for calming anxiety, and otherwise learning to direct one's thoughts. It can also be very challenging, so it's best to start with only a few minutes and then build gradually. The other most common type of meditation is focused meditation, which is almost the opposite. In focused meditation, we direct our thoughts specifically toward an intention, like visualizing an object or contemplating a specific question. A variation on this is to recite a mantra or repeat a prayer or affirmation. This type of meditation is often used in spellcasting and ritual. It's also good for developing visualization skills.

Pathworking

Pathworking is another style of meditation, but it really warrants its own heading and involves a whole bundle of skills that often need to be developed individually. In pathworking—a term which originally comes to us from esoteric Qabalah—the Witch travels inwardly, usually with some kind of guide, to places within the mind's eye for the sake of encountering otherworldly entities, experiencing otherworlds, answering questions, and creating connection with spirits (or sometimes other Witches traveling the same paths). You'll also hear pathworking described as guided meditation, because often we rely on some kind of narrator to describe the paths we're following as we visualize them and also because it's common to invoke personal guardians and guides to accompany us. Pathworking is helpful for generating insight, connecting with others on astral planes, and encountering spirits and gods. It requires strong visualization skills, a good imagination, and the ability to sit or lie in stillness for long periods of time without just falling asleep! There are tons of recordings available online to help you practice pathworking (many for free).

Journaling

The value of journaling really can't be overstated, which is why most books assume you're keeping a notebook close by and advise you to jot down your thoughts and reflect on what you're reading. Aside from working directly with a licensed therapist, journaling is perhaps the best way to explore your inner workings, your patterns, and the nature of your own mind. What starts with recording the mundane details of your day will quickly turn into reflection on your feelings and experiences if you allow it. Journaling also creates space to safely process one's emotions, to vent, and to problem-solve. Years of journals will also establish a record of all your magical work, allowing you to track your growth, pinpoint difficulties, and discern patterns (which you can then change as needed). Conventional journaling is much more difficult than most books will tell you, though. The physical act of writing is more taxing than many realize (especially writers), and it's cultivated over years of practice. The point, however, is reflection, not keeping gorgeous physical books full of pristine handwritten brilliance. It's more than okay to type, to use a voice recorder or dictation software, to speak into a camera, or to scrapbook or make visual art. Do whatever thing allows you to move your thoughts out of your head and put them somewhere you can contemplate them.

Divination

Most Witches learn at least one method of divination as part of their regular practice, which allows them to receive information they might not otherwise have, usually about a particular situation or as a way of generally checking in with what themes or lessons may be present in a given period of time. Lots of Witches perform divination daily, perhaps by pulling a single tarot card or rune and then reflecting on it throughout the day. They might perform more elaborate divination before working a spell, on special days like sabbats, the New Year, or the first day of the month, or when a particularly pressing issue is at hand. All divination requires practice and discernment, and some methods may require quite a lot of study, but this is a skill that is essential in any magical arsenal.

Maintaining a Shrine

A great way to solidify one's connection to a god or spirit is to build a shrine in your home to honor them. The act of tending this space—keeping it clean, making offerings, spending time in contemplation or communion before it—can help you to maintain focus on your spirituality, as well as on any religious obligations you may have. Most Witches have at least one, and many of us have several for different purposes. You might tend a sacred flame here, pour libations for ancestors, pray to a deity, or set up a sacred space for yourself to journal, meditate, or perform divination.

Prayer

Prayer is an excellent method for building and deepening a relationship with a god (and potentially other spirits). Like meditation or divination, prayer can potentially take a number of forms, but always involves establishing an open line of communication, be it through reciting something memorized, speaking from the heart, or even silently calling out and opening a space in which you might share with whatever entity you feel called toward. Some prayers are elaborate and entail performance at specific times, multiple times per day. Some involve tools, like prayer beads. A variation on prayer entails the reciting of personal affirmations, to shift one's thoughts over the course of the day. Prayer makes some Witches uncomfortable, as it may remind them too much of past religious traditions, but it's a simple and profound way to strengthen one's divine relationships and is worth trying if unfamiliar to you.

Study or Reading

Sometimes learning is totally utilitarian, but with the right mindset study can be a devotional practice as well. Setting aside a designated time and space to read relevant books or otherwise to actively engage in acquiring new magical knowledge is beneficial for lots of reasons we'll discuss in the next chapter.

Working Rites

If you're part of a specific tradition, you probably have designated ritual acts that members of your tradition perform regularly. These sorts of things are often the first that people think of when we start thinking about religious practice. They may include devotional rituals to specific gods, seasonal or lunar rites to be performed at designated times, or rites of passage. These will vary by tradition. Eclectic Witches often develop their own unique rites over time or experiment with those from other types of Witchcraft.

———

This is just a smattering of some of the most widely cited things an individual Witch might include in their personal practice. Some might be familiar and already well-established in your life, whereas others may represent new territory. All of them require time to learn and develop, and a few of them have kind of steep learning curves that may necessitate gradual implementation. Go easy on yourself when adopting any one of them for the first time. Remember: better slow and steady. It does no good to overload yourself and get discouraged. Choose things that inspire and challenge you, rather than accepting it at face value every time someone else tells you that in order to be a Witch you have to practice any one specific thing.

• EXERCISE •
Building a Personal Practice

Wherever you are on the path of the Witch, the cultivation of a personal practice is the best thing you can do for yourself. How much you know, how many initiations you have, how naturally skilled you are, and how many resources you have available to you means absolutely nothing if you're not actually putting those things to use. It's time to let go of whatever hang-ups you're struggling with right now and do some Witchcraft.

Remember: the key here is regularity. Your goal should be consistency, not volume. In each of the following exercises, we'll look at the sorts of things you can be doing to take the next step toward a meaningful, powerful practice, which you can then build on as you establish a new routine or get comfortable with regular magical work.

Air

After your initial hurdles—holy crap, Witchcraft is real!—the hardest thing about starting out as a Witch is structuring your Craft in a way that is refueling, is consistent, and allows for meaning to develop and deepen over time. Other religions and spiritual orders have institutions, formal teachers and schools, and even standardized texts and protocol for learning and growing within their traditions. Witches almost never have any of that stuff. Even the most well-established covens are rarely very old and are often based on the teachings and techniques of only a few people. Overwhelmingly, the path of the Witch is a relatively solitary one. You'll be presented with lots of conflicting perspectives, things to learn and to try, and way more advice than you ever wanted or needed. It's practically accomplishment enough just not getting overwhelmed.

Right now, the best thing you can do is to ensure you're putting strong foundations in place and taking consistent steps forward. It's wonderful to explore freely and try your hand at as much as possible, but your task is to choose one thing to be sure you're doing consistently. Pick some element of personal practice that we've discussed—or one you noticed I left out—and hold yourself accountable for doing it a designated number of times per week. Be reasonable here, but also challenge yourself. If you've never journaled before, don't start with multiple pages every day. Money says you'll crash and burn. But can you do one page three days per week? Can you do a couple of sentences every day? Pick a goal that's reasonable for you.

Here are some more ideas:

- Mark every full and new moon with some kind of celebration, prayer, or spell (that's twenty-six rituals per year, on top of any seasonal holidays you celebrate).

- Perform a weekly divination and then reflect on it at the end of the week.
- Set up a shrine to your ancestors, to a deity, or to the spirit of your home. When you come home from work or school every day, take five minutes to say hello, share a drink, and reflect on the day.
- Quiet your mind through meditation for five minutes before going to bed (or before getting out of bed).
- Keep a dream journal by your bed and record what you remember of your dreams every day.
- Compose a set of three to five affirmations and recite them at your altar or in front of a mirror before you begin your routine each day.

I could keep going here. But just pick one thing! You may experience the temptation to choose more—don't. Let whatever else you want come and go, but choose one task to maintain. When that feels easy and natural—perhaps after several months—add something additional. Build your practice gradually, and it will serve you more completely.

Fire

Some of the things that get in the way of regular practice for lots of Witches are travel, working within an irregular schedule, and not having designated private space for Craft work because you have to share or otherwise live in close quarters. A good solution for all of these—and one I've used for years—is to make and enchant a Witch's ladder to carry in your purse or pocket when you're on the go. These simple tools have many functions. Essentially, they are simply pieces of string or cord with knots tied into them, sometimes holding charms or tokens. Sometimes, they're made from multiple strings braided together, with each strand representing something specific.

The Witch's ladder can be used for spellcasting—in which your intentions are held by tying knots and then released in the untying—but it can also function as a kind of altar, containing representations of each element, your deities, or whatever other symbols are important to you. Creating sacred space, or even casting a circle, could be a simple matter of pulling out your Witch's ladder and arranging it on a flat surface, depending on how long you decide to make it.

I use my own Witch's ladder the way some Witches use prayer beads. I've woven several strands of different colors together, then tied in several charms at equal points in the braid: a piece of amber, a silver pentacle, a fox vertebrae, an agate carved with a rune, and a few other personal tokens. Each represents something important to my Craft, and I've composed prayers to recite that correspond to each. Simply holding it in my hands, handling each charm, and reciting ingrained words in succession is enough to put me into an altered state and open the door for otherworldly encounters.

Making a Witch's ladder can be as simple or complex as you'd like. Build meaning into every component. Choose special colors and materials. Tie knots in it that represent commitments you've made or goals you're working toward. Incorporate tokens that speak to what makes your Craft unique and personal. When you're finished, consecrate the entire thing. Carry it when you travel, handle it often, pray with it, cast spells with it, and use it as a lifeline when you're feeling a need for connection.

Water

This exercise is deceptively simple, but it is ideal for anyone who needs to refocus and go deeper, while also developing their observation skills and their relationship with the world outside of themselves, especially when life gets stressful. All you're going to do is care for a plant!

If you have the space to do so and access to a pot and appropriate soil, it is best to grow one from seed. You may choose any plant you like, but if you're new to gardening I would recommend you pick something relatively easy: any type of bean, squashes, peppers, basil, chamomile, calendula, and mint will all grow readily from seed, with minimal preparation. If you already have some skill with growing things, choose something that requires a bit more care, or choose a plant that you would like to also build a spiritual alliance with as well.

Growing a plant—even an easy one—requires care and attention, and will force you out of your own head on a daily basis as you water and tend to it. Talk to it, meditate with it, monitor its soil pH and moisture, and also keep a daily record of its growth. No matter where your personal practice is in this moment, tending to another living thing will require that you kick it up a notch. As it progresses in its lifecycle, you will also learn how to foster it, how to safely harvest it, and how to use whatever parts you collect. This is a practical skill, but your focus here is developing your awareness, your attentiveness, and your connection to something outside of yourself. Plants are excellent at teaching patience, improvisation, and an appreciation for slow progress.

If you can't grow something from seed, it's okay to take a cutting. Some houseplants may be well-suited to this project too, though it would be best to choose something young and small rather than a mature plant. I've also done this exercise with trees living outside. Choose an individual tree and spend the year closely documenting its growth, the changes it undergoes, the animals that inhabit it, and how it survives where it does. When does it flower and fruit? How does it disperse its seeds?

Who knows—you might develop an interest in plants in general and their magical properties. You might end up with a whole garden on your hands. But there's something inherently magical about plants, and especially about encouraging life through your own actions, that does wonders for a personal practice as a whole.

Earth

Okay. You've been at this for a long time. You're in a rut. I know.

But I'd bet anything there's a thing you know full well you aren't doing the way you should be. What is it?

We've all got that one thing. That thing that every single teacher we've had, and every book we've read says we need to be doing…but we just don't. For me, that thing is meditation. I'm the queen of coming up with excuses for why I don't do it the way I know I should: I'm tired, I'm busy, I can't focus, it's hard, it's boring, my back hurts, my leg's asleep, I don't really need this, meditation doesn't work for me, whatever.

What's your thing that you don't do, and you tell yourself it's because you don't need to or it doesn't really help you? Meditation is the answer I hear the most frequently, but journaling is another popular one. Other popular choices are marking the new moon, celebrating every sabbat, keeping a dream journal, doing daily devotions, or checking in consistently with students, an initiator, or a teacher.

Your task is to flip back and complete the task for Air, but without the option: you have to choose that one thing that you aren't doing that you have a litany of excuses about. Treat it like it's brand new, and use the same strategies that I've suggested to beginners: small steps, short periods of time, accommodations where necessary, and being gentle with yourself.

Chapter 6
Study

My very first Witchcraft teacher was a high priestess in the Blue Star tradition of Wicca. I had been teaching myself from books and the internet for several years at that point and had gotten to where I felt like I had gone as far as I could on my own. Every book I read felt like the same book, and most of what I found online was just recycled from the same few sources and posted without either reference or thought. I was committed to practicing the Craft, and I wanted to do so deeply, thoroughly, and properly, if there was such a thing. I knew that some of the oldest styles of Witchcraft—and traditional Wicca in particular, for that had always been my focus—were intended to be practiced in groups, with a formal training system that brought in candidates through initiation or adoption into a specific lineage. So I began seeking a teacher who could bring me into such a lineage. Who could teach me the things I couldn't find in books.

I met her at a local chain restaurant after weeks of corresponding through email. Most of the Witches and Pagans I'd met at that point were youngsters like myself, inspired to pursue Witchcraft through a combination of deep childhood longing for magic and the encouragement of the latest wave of media Witches and popular Pagan books (the nineties were a fantastic decade for both). Here was one of the first true adults I'd met, with a practice going back to another decade, another region, and within a specific tradition. I was prepared to gobble everything she was willing to teach me (and, lucky me, she was wonderful). And her first lesson? Her first lesson was that this was a religion with homework!

The idea that Witchcraft—whether it is a specific tradition or not—requires study is not unique to a formal coven or teacher-student relationship. Witches of all kinds are quick to dole out recommended reading lists upon request, and all over social media we find people referencing their studies. Witches are often great readers, and as a community, we tend to look to authors as our primary guides. Everywhere there is the assertion that we must be constantly studying, learning more. In the age of the internet, you now have an overwhelming number of correspondence courses you could sign up for, on everything from beginning Witchcraft to divination, herbalism to sex magic, and even starting your own Witchy business. There is a potentially infinite amount of content you could consume, in any medium you could name. Some traditions have specific curricula that students must work through, completing research projects, formal papers, and other assessments that you may have thought you'd left back in school. But even Witchcrafts that aren't so formally structured practically always carry with them the assumption that you are always learning.

On the one hand, knowing that there is always more to learn can be exciting and motivating. On the other, it is easy to become overwhelmed, discouraged, or just plain stuck. How do you choose when you have infinite choices? How do you push forward when you feel like it's all just the same crap over and over again, in every book, every social media post, and every festival workshop? And why do we feel the need to bury ourselves in intellectual pursuits when Witchcraft is so fundamentally about practice, connections, and experiencing things out in the world? Do you even need teachers? And how would you go about finding a worthwhile one, when everyone seems to be claiming expertise and is more than happy to take your money? Finally, if you've been living this path for decades, is there really anything left to learn?

In this chapter, we'll take a hard look at the relationship between study and practice and where they do and don't align. We'll discuss strategies for pushing your magical education forward, no matter how much you already know. And while I'm a devoted book lover, we'll also put books aside for a bit and consider other important techniques for learning more and deepening your personal practice.

The Relationship between Study and Practice

Many spiritual traditions advocate that practitioners and devotees spend at least some of their time in study. For Christianity, this usually means the careful reading of the Gospels. All over the world, evangelical Protestants encourage their children to memorize lengthy passages from the Bible so that the word of God is always close at hand. Jewish children, whatever their native language, often study Hebrew so that they can read the Torah, and they do so before their communities when they come of age as part of the ritual of Bar or Bat Mitzvah. Both Catholics and Buddhists are renowned historically for a dedication to text and institutional education, with specialized orders of devotees who dedicate their lives to both interpretation and propagation of sacred knowledge. Indeed, the power of study, books, and the abilities to read and write are so powerful—so sacred—that they have historically been denied to certain groups of people in order to preserve established power structures. Women, people of color, and the poor have at times been excluded from education, denied access to literacy, and tortured and murdered for pursuing it anyway. One need look no further than the disparity still present in American public schools to see that we are still living in a time when education—who gets it and who doesn't—is contested. Cheesy and harmless as it may have sounded in grade school, the message is deadly true: knowledge is power. And part of what you're doing as a Witch, whatever kind you are, is building your power.

For Witchcraft traditions with roots in Western European occultism, the drive to study isn't only about religious devotion. Magic was and continues to be defined as a science as much as a spiritual practice. For Éliphas Lévi, it was science that served as the foundation of magic, and part of the work of the magus included the unification of reason and faith. Lévi charged candidates for initiation to master themselves and their surroundings through study. In *Transcendental Magic*, he tells us that, "To attain...the knowledge and power of the Magi, there are four indispensable conditions—an intelligence illuminated by study, an intrepidity which nothing can check, a will which cannot be broken, and a prudence which nothing can corrupt and nothing intoxicate."[22] You may recognize this admonition as the Witch's Pyramid: to know, to dare, to will, and to be silent. The first is to *know*.

The understanding of Witchcraft as a science, either in addition to a religion or sometimes as a secular pursuit, continues among contemporary practitioners. Writers like Laurie Cabot, Silver RavenWolf, and Christopher Penczak have used similar language. Penczak most clearly approaches the Craft with a skeptical mind initially, telling us, "For the longest time, I ignored other facets of the definition of Witchcraft, namely art and religion. I focused on the science of the Craft. I looked at Witchcraft as an experiment."[23] In other words, even where we may think of Witchcraft as religion, spirituality, or art, it is also operative (and perhaps primarily so). It is a thing that we must go out and do, and this first entails study and then experimentation. We have to learn *how*. Penczak, like many of today's magical teachers, goes on to describe the significance that studying other sciences—especially quantum physics—can have for the developing Witch. This perspective is not unusual in Witchcrafts influenced by Western European occultism.

For Witches outside of direct sight of the Western Mystery Tradition, one may be less likely to hear this usage of "science" to describe the work of the Witch, but the emphasis on study is no less apparent. Practitioners who see their tradition as a craft alone still work to master magical correspondences, to become familiar with the local flora and fauna, to learn the finer points of herbalism, and train in other Witcheries. There is always more to learn, whether from books; through direct contact with the land, spirits, other Witches; or through more otherworldly means.

Truly, knowledge is critical for all of us, because knowledge is the doorway through which we acquire and then develop the power of the Witch. As a magician, the more you know, the more flexible you can be. Don't have everything you need for a working on hand? A mastery of

---

22. Éliphas Lévi, *Transcendental Magic: Its Doctrine and Ritual*, trans. Arthur Edward Waite (London: Bracken Books, 1995), 37.

23. Christopher Penczak, *The Inner Temple of Witchcraft: Magick, Meditation, and Psychic Development* (St. Paul, MN: Llewellyn Publications, 2002), 10.

a wide variety of correspondences will allow you to make effective substitutions. Want to maximize the likelihood of your spells working as intended? Incorporate precise magical timing that takes the moon phase, the day of the week, and astrological conditions into consideration. Want to be able to interpret ancient or medieval magical texts for yourself? Learn to read Greek, Hebrew, French, or Latin. Do you know when your traditions were born and what histories shaped them? This will give you context and build conviction. Are you familiar with other traditions? This will allow for comparison, which builds honesty and makes it easier to recognize inconsistencies, ineffectiveness, or even injustice in your practice. We could go on and on—there is always more to know, and all of it is potentially useful in developing as a Witch.

There's a balance to be struck here, however. Study must fuel practice, not overshadow or replace it. Knowing histories and being able to recite passages from medieval grimoires won't by themselves make you a Witch, and a large book collection is not a sure sign of an effective or a devoted magician. You have to take what you read and put it into practice somehow. If that knowledge never leaves your head—if you don't experiment with it, put it to work, reform it into your own, use it to change yourself for the better—you are missing its purpose and won't move forward in your practice. This is a trap that many Witches fall into at some point. We tend to love books, and with so many available and so much care required to balance our spiritual lives with everything else going on from day to day, it's easy to find yourself becoming an armchair Witch. Reading and study may be part of practice, but they cannot be the only part.

Over the course of your magical life, in fact, you will likely find that your most valuable lessons won't come from books at all. You'll meet and learn from others in your community, whether that means casual online acquaintances or formal relationships with established teachers or traditions. You'll learn from the land you call home and also from any gods or spirits you meet. You'll also have individual, personal moments of inspiration or revelation, in which you'll be struck by ideas inspired by forces so subtle they'll feel like they come from nowhere. In the following sections, we'll talk a lot about text and how to get the most out of reading, but learning isn't only about books. It's about mindset too.

Beginner's Mind

I'm kind of jealous of people who are just now beginning their pursuit of the Craft. I can remember when I first discovered magic, Paganism, Witchcraft, the gods...all of it. It was the most exciting time of my life, better than first love, going to college, or starting my first career. Learning that Witchcraft was real and that, if I wanted to, I could become a Witch, was like stumbling into another world that existed parallel to the one I was living in. Every day, every book, every new technique, every spell and prayer was an assurance of more to come. Over time, that excitement would wax and wane. My rosy, newfound love was sometimes diminished by harsh experiences in public Witch spaces. Not everyone was supportive, and over the years I would meet people who were prejudiced, elitist, cruel, or even predatory. I also just hit walls, which is a normal experience on any magical path! Sometimes I'd put a lot of effort into a ritual and it would fall flat. I'd feel like my gods weren't responding to me. Spells wouldn't work out the way I wanted, or I would struggle with whatever new technique I was trying to learn. Other times, other parts of my life would just get in the way and I would lose focus or feel disconnected. Over years of practice, I've developed habits (both good and bad), preferences and prejudices, and expectations that sometimes create dissatisfaction. In the beginning, however, I was totally open, excited, and thrilled by the possibility that felt infinite in everything I learned and experienced. Even when I would get overwhelmed by how much there was to learn, it always felt like an adventure.

In Zen Buddhism, we find the concept of *shoshin* (初心), which is usually translated as "beginner's mind." Popularized for Western audiences by Shunryu Suzuki (1905–1971) in the 1970s, beginner's mind is a state of openness that we may consciously adopt when we approach a learning experience. Prior knowledge and experiences can actually get in the way of how we study, how we cope with change, and how well we integrate new information. We are often weighed down by our assumptions and established perspectives, even without realizing it. Beginners, however, tend to be more open to possibility. They are hopeful and excited, rather than skeptical or wary. Someone with a beginner's mind has cultivated this outlook, whether or not they are actually a beginner.

Before we discuss resources or techniques, it is worth addressing mindset, and while it is certainly easier said than done, I'm going to ask that you begin with beginner's mind. If you genuinely are a beginner, then rejoice in this wonderful phase of your Witchcraft practice! Once you get your footing, your magical education will likely never be as all-encompassing and as freely flowing again. There will always be more to learn, but never again will you have as much, in this moment. If you are an old hand, tired, cynical, and even a bit jaded, I want you to pause for a while and reflect on what it felt like to be new. Remember the excitement of your first book? The first time you had the chance to speak to another Witch? Before bad experiences ground you down, and before negative people revealed a side of the wider community that you didn't know was there?

Every time you crack open a new book, show up for a new workshop or festival, take a new class, or surf into a new online community, consciously pause and put yourself into a beginner's mindset. Imagine that there is something new to discover (because there always is, as we shall see later), and that this will take you one step farther on your path (because it surely will). When we adopt beginner's mind, we put our expectations and assumptions aside. What we see depends so much on what we look for, and when we have expectations—especially cynical expectations—our experiences often become self-fulfilling prophecies. Moving forward, keep that openness and allow yourself to be surprised. You will learn more this way!

How to Choose Better Books
(and Get More Out of the Rest)

Most of us, no matter where we are in our Craft, started with books. The very first time I heard about modern Witches, I was pawing through an old box of books in my grandfather's attic and came across a sensationalist Time Life title full of nude and seminude pictures of magical luminaries like Janet Farrar, Maxine and Alex Sanders, and Patricia Crowther. The nudity alone would have been enough to catch my adolescent interest, but they were clearly up to something incredible, with their ritual blades, circles inscribed on the ground, spooky masks, and serene, beautiful faces. It would be another few years before I read my first book about how to practice Witchcraft myself, but I never forgot those images (and I still have the book!). Books are gateways. For most of us, they're our best and only teachers.

Only a few decades ago, books were comparatively difficult to come by, and choices were limited. My elders got their books through mail order-catalogs, bought them from specialty stores on trips to the big city, or lucked into them secondhand at discount shops. I had the luxury of choosing mine from among the ten or so possible options at the mall's Waldenbooks, sandwiched between the titles on the spiritual dangers of playing Magic: The Gathering and true stories from alien abductees. When eBay became a thing, my friend Rachel used her dad's credit card to help me buy a copy of Gerald Gardner's *Witchcraft Today*. Today, new Witches have literally thousands of choices and can access most of them from the relative privacy of their phones and computers. Public libraries can get you many titles through interlibrary loan for free. More and more Witchy writers release new books every single day. We are living in a golden age of magical publishing. But how the hell do you choose?

No one wants to waste their time and money on books that aren't worth the paper they're printed on, but how can you be sure you're finding the good ones and avoiding the duds? There's no 100-percent, surefire guarantee, but here are some strategies that will dramatically improve the odds of being happier with your choices:

1. Narrow Your Focus and Be Clear about Your Goals as a Reader

With so many books to choose from, it's useful to remember that there is an extraordinary amount of variety, as well. There is no singular "Witchcraft" that one must study and no one way to do anything. There's a lot to be said for simply browsing and stumbling into subjects that look interesting, but if you really want to get the most bang for your buck (and your time), get specific about what you want to learn and why. The answer probably isn't another generic book about Witchcraft, written for newcomers. What are you *actually* looking to learn? Do you want to read about the Witch trials in Germany? Do you want to learn how to make and use flying ointment? How to divine with a crystal ball? Would you like to learn more about a particular deity or spirit? Do you want to beef up your spellcrafting skills? Are you curious when the stang developed as a tool in Traditional Witchcraft, or what sources Gerald Gardner was using when he was developing the first Wiccan covens? Get as specific as you can, and then work back out as you need to. There are enough people producing books today that there's a good chance you can find someone writing about that niche thing that has piqued your interest.

2. Look beyond the Hype

Sometimes popular books are popular because they're genuinely awesome, but sometimes they're popular because they have a team of savvy marketers and a larger-than-average promotional budget backing them. Read what you can, of course, but don't be afraid to consider books that aren't on the best-sellers list. Just because the author doesn't have a giant social media platform doesn't mean they aren't a brilliant Witch and writer. When searching for books, look at small presses, self-published books, and books that may be a few pages down in your internet searches. Often, the more advanced books, the deeper books, and the more niche books have smaller audiences (because there are more beginners than there are old-timers), so they don't get as much attention from bloggers, reviewers, publishers, or influencers.

3. Turn the Author into the Subject

The truth is that most books are just. . .pretty okay. Average is average for a reason, after all, and collectively we do a lot of rehashing old ideas, repackaging established techniques, and recycling old narratives. We've come a long way as a movement, but most books just aren't going to dramatically change your life the way you might want them to. You're going to find yourself reading books that just aren't as awesome as you were hoping. The good news is that they can still teach you something, if you let them. At the very least, every book tells you something about the person writing it: what their values were, what perspectives they held, what moment they were living in, and what their personal practice probably looked like. Over time, these personal reflections become our collective history. Turn the author into the subject of the book so that at least you can glean some insight into another Witch's life. And look for those nuggets of wisdom and useful advice—over time those will add up.

4. Reverse Engineer a Reading List

Many books now contain bibliographies, works cited pages, or recommended reading lists. Use these where they exist. If you enjoyed a book and you aren't sure where to go next, check out the books that author referred to as they were writing their own. Keep in mind that a citation is *not* an endorsement—it only means that the author needed to address an idea contained in that text, not that they're in agreement with it. If the author doesn't provide citations or a recommended reading list, be mindful of where they reference other authors and books within the text. The very first book I ever read about Wicca, *Teen Witch* by Silver RavenWolf, included a passing reference to *Diary of a Witch* by Sybil Leek. Reading Sybil Leek led me to Gerald Gardner and Aleister Crowley, who then led me to James Frazer and Margaret Murray. Here, in this introductory book aimed at teenagers, I found clues that led me to deeper and more complex places than anyone probably intended. When an author points you elsewhere, follow the lead. You will never run out of books.

Advanced Books versus Advanced Readers

"Where are the advanced books?" the people cry from the streets. On every message board, social media outlet, and at every gathering, this singular complaint rises to the fore of our magical literary discussions. Collectively, our modern movement is, conservatively, a few decades shy of a hundred years old, and yet it sometimes seems as though we've failed to go any deeper than the basics. Popular books mostly rehash the same histories, the same perspectives, and the same techniques, some of which weren't that great the first time we read them. There's got to be more out there, right? Who needs one more slick, hashtag-worthy Witch book that doesn't get beyond how to cast a circle and the magical properties of citrine? Where's the *real* stuff? The *deep* stuff?

I know, I know. I've made similar lamentations in the past. When you've been around for a few years—or if you're just a voracious reader—it can very quickly feel like you're just reading the same book over and over.

There's lots of good news, though. First, as we discussed in the previous section, there are more books available now than ever, and this is good for all kinds of Witches. Thanks to independent publishing, artisanal publishing, and self-publishing, it's easier than ever for more writers to get their work out there and be heard (and that's even before we factor in bloggers, podcasters, vloggers, and other types of content creators). If you're reading the same material over and over from books that look the same and are being marketed to the same people, then the problem isn't the books. The problem is *where* you're buying books and *who* you're taking recommendations from. Use the techniques in the previous section to search more effectively for appropriate reading material. Branch out from mainstream sellers, best-sellers, and well-established authors. Give academic works a try. Check out specialty occult presses and antiquarian book dealers. Search online artist markets for zines. The problem isn't that deeper, more specialized Witchcraft titles aren't being written; the problem is that readers don't know where to look for them. You are no longer such a reader.

Second, there is a huge difference between being able to acquire an advanced book and actually being an advanced reader. Your goal should be the latter, for this will serve you much better throughout your life and keep you from becoming the dreaded armchair Witch. What do I mean by advanced reader? Let me explain with a lesson learned from my days as a classroom teacher.

When I started working as an English teacher for high school students, I very quickly discovered that literacy and the ability to read are not the same thing. Many of my students could read fluently. We could read passages from novels or textbooks out loud, they could answer questions about what was happening, and they were all champs at locating key vocabulary, significant dates, and quotes that were likely to show up on quizzes and tests. But when asked to identify theme, to make connections with other texts, and to discuss meaning and application, many students (most, in fact) started to flounder. I had seen the same thing years before when I was a university lecturer. Students—all of them adults, and some of them in their third or fourth year of study—could regurgitate professor-approved interpretations of reading assignments, but with an uncomfortable level of frequency could not assimilate readings to derive deeper meaning or reach original conclusions. To be crystal clear, these people were *not* intellectually incapable or uneducated. My high schoolers were *not* all lazy or disinterested. Plenty of them were straight-A students who were committed to their educations. The problem was that, over the course of their school lives, we'd all collectively mistaken reading and writing for literacy itself.

An advanced reader is a *literate* reader, who actively builds intellectual connections, maintains an inner dialogue with text, is capable of detecting subtext, and can take what they're reading and apply it to their own relationships with the world. Before we ever arrive at what people call "critical reading," we must first have understanding and engagement. And these abilities should never be taken for granted. They are difficult to teach, difficult to acquire, and widely not even available, especially to marginalized students.

Even if you are an advanced reader with a high command of literacy, there's a fair chance you're not always choosing to put those skills to work. It's fine to read just for the sake of reading and to periodically turn down your intellect to enjoy some brain candy, but if you're really trying to learn something, there are some basic strategies you should be regularly employing.

The first and most fundamental technique is something teachers call active reading, and it's exactly what it sounds like: reading while actively engaging with the text. You know that voice in your head that responds to books and movies (and, well, pretty much everything) with statements like "I wonder what's going to happen next," or "Wow, I didn't know that," or "I don't think I agree with that"? Keeping track of that voice is a great way to observe your thoughts and interact with what you're reading. For years, I told my students to keep sticky notes on hand to record that inner voice as they read. If you own the book you're reading, you can also write in the margins. It's a small thing, but you'll remember more and build connections more easily.

For this reason, it's always a good idea to read with a pen or pencil in hand. Not a highlighter! The act of physically making notes and recording your on-the-spot thoughts is widely demonstrated to be more conducive to learning than highlighting, which doesn't engage the brain the way so many of us seem to think it does.[24] Your notes could consist of your inner voice, quotes that stand out to you, things you aren't sure about and want to cross-reference, questions you want to contemplate or pose to others, or even rants about how much you hate what you're reading. So long as you're engaged! This, by the way, is also sure to make your reading *slower*. It's easy to get caught up in the impulse to read as much as you can, as fast as you can. People all over social media take on reading challenges to rack up scores of titles annually, and many of us are quick to show off book collections and boast about how much and how fast we read, but never mistake speed and volume for thoroughness. If you have to choose between reading fast and reading well, choose the latter.

Finally—and this is key—reading a magical book and working through the lessons of a book are dramatically different things. Many of us, myself included, have bemoaned that books repeat each other, that they all contain the same advice, or that they're too remedial, but how many readers actually work though books as the author intended? Being told to meditate every day, or to practice visualization exercises, or to establish a daily altar devotion may seem repetitive and easy. Until we actually *do* it.

I'll use myself as an example here. Many years ago, when I was still relatively new to Witchcraft, I bought a popular book that purported to be a year and a day's worth of study. Each chapter was only a few pages long, the author was approachable and well-regarded, and I did what a lot of readers do (maybe most readers): I read the whole thing in a couple of weeks and called myself done. The chapters were short, but they contained exercises, rituals, meditations, and journaling prompts—but, well, I kind of just skimmed over those (I could just come back to them later if I wanted, right?). I liked the author's perspective and I picked up some tidbits along the way, but mostly I filed it away in my head as a good resource, or perhaps something I could recommend to people less experienced than myself. I did

---

24. For more on the ineffectiveness of highlighting and other study techniques, consider John Dunlosky et al., "Improving Students' Learning with Effective Learning Techniques: Promising Directions from Cognitive and Educational Psychology," *Psychological Science in the Public Interest* 14, no. 1 (January 2013): 4–58.

a couple of the first activities, but then I moved onto the next book in the series. No big deal.

Years later, I signed up to take a class that used this same book as a textbook. I wanted to explore other styles of Craft, I was in a bit of a rut, and I thought what the hell. Why not? Let me tell you something. Working through every exercise in that same book, month by month, building from one chapter to the next, and taking the time to engage with the book as the author actually intended was a *completely* different experience. And it wasn't just because I was part of a class but because I was actually holding myself accountable. I set down the piece of my ego that told me I already knew all this stuff, and I realized that for years I hadn't actually been *doing* all the things my beginner books had been advising.

How many times have you read through a book but only skimmed the exercises? Maybe you're doing it to this one right now. If you're only curious or just looking to explore casually, that's cool. But if you want to grow as a Witch, you have to *do*. The doing is often the difference between a beginner book and an advanced book. The material is rarely all that different. Instead, it's the mindset and commitment of the reader.

Many Ways to Learn

Up to this point, we've mostly discussed books. Even in the digital age, it seems like that's the medium people turn to first, but it's certainly not the only one, and it may not even be the best one depending on your resources and how you prefer to learn. The sheer volume of blogs, articles, forums, social media accounts, and websites on Witchcraft, Paganism, magic, and the occult is staggering, and seems to increase exponentially every couple of years. Many established authors maintain internet platforms to augment the content of their books, while thousands of other kinds of community leaders—tradition heads, teachers, clergy, event organizers—create all manner of learning resources, from videos to ritual databases, podcasts to discussion communities. Much of this for free. On top of all that, you can also find correspondence courses, which may involve one-on-one attention from an established teacher, involvement in an exclusive community, a self-paced series of lessons completed online, or even correspondence through the mail.

And of course there are in-person opportunities available to many student Witches as well! If you live near a metaphysical or occult shop, ask if they offer classes or workshops. Many do, and some even stream them online so that you don't have to be local to take advantage. You may also seek out another, more experienced Witch to study under or pursue training with a traditional-style coven, or at least a coven that is open to teaching newcomers.[25] If you are able, consider attending festivals, Pagan Pride Day, and other kinds of magical events, even if they are not specifically aimed at Witches (there is a great deal of crossover in magical communities, and you are sure to meet all kinds of practitioners). Reach out to your favorite authors on social media and see if they offer workshops through live-streaming or on video platforms like YouTube. Increasingly, many do!

If you practice Witchcraft for any length of time, you're sure to explore many modes of education. You may already have a favorite. I've done all of these myself, and each has its merits and drawbacks. Many people insist they're only one type of learner or only one type of Witch, but most actually benefit from a variety of strategies in multiple environments, all employed at the same time. Read books *and* learn from teachers and peers. Build a solitary practice *and* experiment with a group. Turn to internet communities *and* local communities. What they say is certainly true: books can't teach you Witchcraft by themselves, and you won't read everything in books. But it's equally true that no one teacher knows everything and no one tradition or magical system has all the answers. So cast a wide net. Never stop being a student.

Unlearning

It can be tricky hunting for advice from other Witches, especially on social media. There are a lot of cynics out there who paint a dire picture of the quality of information circulating in Witchcraft spaces. Maybe you've heard from them about all the dangerously bad books that are

---

25. If you're interested in pursuing training with a coven, consider reading my earlier work, *Traditional Wicca: A Seeker's Guide* (Llewellyn, 2018). This book is specifically geared toward initiatory styles of Wicca, but large potions of the practical advice apply to Witch, Pagan, and magical groups as a whole.

supposedly out there. There are even more bad blogs, bad channels, and bad social media posts, they say. There's just *badness* all around, making it impossible for anyone to really learn anything genuine. False teachings, incorrect history, shoddy magical techniques, misinterpretations of traditional material, and goodness knows what else. How on earth can anyone be expected to get off on the right foot and learn things correctly when they have to wade through a cesspool of misinformation, both online and on bookstore shelves? If only everything was peer reviewed, or curated by experts. If only publishers would stop appealing to the lowest common denominator, come the angry cries. If only beginner witches would get off social media, get serious, and *do the work*. Am I right, or am I right?

It sounds kind of silly when I actually write it down like that, and it should. This is a lot of melodrama and fearmongering. Still, these are some very common anxieties in Witchcraft communities. They often leave beginners to worry that they're going to read a book that's full of misinformation and that it's going to hobble their progress in the Craft. Meanwhile, covenleaders and Witchcraft teachers worry that they're going to wind up with students who've been exposed to that misinformation, and then they're going to have to help them "unlearn" something. Practically everywhere you look there are Witches in public spaces complaining about how damaging the wrong book can be. We talk about authors leading people astray or social media influencers ruining the next generation of practitioners, but it's time to chill out and put things in perspective.

When I first came to the Craft, I read books that more experienced practitioners told me were going to ruin my later experiences as a Witch. I was told that I wasn't serious because I was learning from Witchcraft books that were aimed at young people, and that made Witchcraft seem easy and approachable (lots of people seem to think Witchcraft is only authentic when it's difficult and painful). This wasn't serious Witchcraft, people said to me. I read histories online that I later found out were untrue, and I experimented with magical philosophies and systems that weren't very effective. I met a lot of people over the years who gave me advice that turned out to be wrong or unhelpful. I also made a ton of mistakes when it came to my public behavior, how I interacted with my elders and fellow seekers, and, later, how I ran a coven and taught within my own tradition.

It was all part of a process. Learning takes time, and it's not simply a matter of reading the "correct" books, getting the "real" training, or knowing the "right" people. It's a mixed bag, pretty much anywhere you look.

The fear that you (or your students) will read a problematic book that will create more work later in the form of "unlearning" may seem like a reasonable concern, but it's not a helpful place to dwell. You're going to read problematic books! You just *will*. You're going to consume media that ends up not serving you in the long run, or that you'll enjoy at the time and then question as you gain more experience. You'll think some piece of history is 100 percent factual, and then new research will come out that will totally raze your worldview. Learn to be *excited* when this happens and not discouraged.

When I was in the ninth grade, another kid in my chemistry class asked our teacher how he would feel if some new scientific knowledge came out that rendered the periodic table of elements obsolete. My chemistry teacher—who was the best, by the way—said, "That would be incredible! It would mean that humanity was making progress. And wouldn't it be exciting to get to learn something brand new?"

That's exactly how I felt when I graduated from my beginner Wicca books and began reading scholarly works on Witchcraft, books of ceremonial magic, and books on Wiccan theology and tradition. Everyone needs to start somewhere, and what seems "bad" to you may be exactly what someone else needs to take the next step forward. Does that mean that every book and blog post gets a free pass from critique? No, of course not! But critique the *content*, not the person who is consuming it without another point of reference. It's perfectly possible to read something questionable and not be "ruined" by it (and reading only really great books, by the way, is not an assurance of wisdom or moral character).

If you're in a position of authority, consume widely and disseminate those materials that you feel are the most accurate and helpful, and do so without allowing your ego to lead you to believe that you already know everything and can't learn from contemporary voices. If you're a newcomer, read with discernment and apply the same kinds of tests that you might use when evaluating other sources outside of the Witchcraft community (whether teachers, courses, social media pages, or books). You might be new to Witchcraft, but you're probably *not* new to figuring out when someone has an agenda that doesn't align with yours, when it's time to look for a second opinion, and when a text is inherently problematic (racist, sexist, transphobic, or otherwise worthy of the dumpster out back). Use those skills you've already developed elsewhere just by being a thinking person out in the world.

Learning is an ongoing process. You don't "unlearn" things—you analyze why they were meaningful at the time and what should change, and then you take the next step forward. That's all any of us can do.

Keeping It All in Perspective

At this point, it's worth reminding ourselves what the purpose of all this studying really is. We understand, of course, that knowledge is valuable. The more you learn and understand, the more flexible you can be in your practice, and the more tools you have at your disposal. Far be it from me to tell anyone that they shouldn't be reading or actively trying to learn new skills, or doing what they can to better understand their histories and traditions. There's a trap here, though, and one that's too frequently overlooked.

It's often said that Witchcraft is work. Everywhere it seems we see Witches admonishing newcomers to "do the work" or praising longstanding leaders and teachers for "having done the work." At this point in this book, you should have a better idea of what "the work" actually entails. Much of it is emotional—internal and difficult to fully articulate. Too often, "the work" is taken in an overly literal sense, turning your personal practice of Witchcraft into something more akin to a job or to school. It's deceptively easy to find yourself in a place where you are treating your studies as though they themselves are the point. The Craft becomes a contest (with yourself or with the imaginings you have about other Witches) for how much time you can spend reading, memorizing, assembling an elaborate book of shadows or grimoire, making social media posts about what you're learning, and maybe even blogging or teaching others, online or in a coven setting.

Culturally, there is an enormous amount of pressure on each of us to turn what we love—our passions, our spiritualities, our art—into something that's profitable, or otherwise contributes in some measurable way to improving society or the lives of other people. Capitalism and the Protestant work ethic—whether or not we are capitalists or Protestants—hum in the background of many societies, so imperceptibly that we forget they're there, woven into the wider culture, especially in the United States. Both raise us to believe that we must be productive at all times, that work is inherently valuable regardless of what you're producing (as long as it's profitable, in capitalism's case), and to feel guilty when you find yourself with too much free time on your hands. What would our communities look like if we told each other that Witchcraft was joy instead of work? What if we stopped relying on the ableist perspective that every Witch needs to be a scholar, or even a reader?

To advance one's spiritual practice *is* admirable. Many magical systems have extensive curricula, down to accepted reading lists and examinations. These have their place and call to many. But Witchcraft as a whole largely concerns itself with practical application, with a heavy focus on improving the practitioner's circumstances and building useful, deep connections to the world around us. Much of your development will be intangible, reflected in altered perspectives, deeper understandings, and more control over your personal power. None of these things neatly correlates with how many books you can read in a year or how thoroughly you can take notes. It is necessary to take time to integrate what we learn and to put it into practice. This sometimes means time away from study.

"A field needs to lie fallow sometimes in order to replenish itself and support the next season of growth," my friend Frater A said to me one afternoon over coffee. Frater A is a Thelemite magician, accustomed to long reading lists and regular check-ins with mentors. We'd been chatting about our own experiences feeling overwhelmed by how much there is to learn in our respective traditions. Normally, reading and writing about the Craft makes me feel excited, but lately I'd been experiencing burnout. What Frater A said really struck me, and now when I sit down to study, I remind myself of why I began practicing in the first place, and how this is or isn't in line with those ultimate goals: connection, love, touching something greater than myself, building meaning, improving my own life, and helping those around me.

So study. Read. Watch videos and listen to podcasts. Share info posts on social media. Learn. But keep your ultimate purpose in mind and allow yourself to enjoy periods spent lying fallow, processing and integrating what you're learning into a practice that truly serves you. There's no test at the end, and no way to read it all and know it all. Resist the urge to compare yourself to another Witch's progress. And if you find yourself feeling guilty for not progressing intellectually at the rate you think you should, question the source of that expectation. Is it truly coming from you and your own needs, or is it the voice of a wider culture with a different agenda in mind? Learn to study well, and take joy in learning, but balance this with practice, and remind yourself over and over why you came here to begin with.

• EXERCISE •
Study Skills

It's always worthwhile to pick up some additional learning strategies, no matter where you are in your practice. For beginners, that may mean how to evaluate a book when you aren't sure what's reliable, or perhaps how to maximize the learning potential of your social media feed. For more experienced Witches, the order of the day may be kindling an interest in some new aspect of Witchcraft, or learning how to cut yourself some slack and just enjoy how much you already know.

Air

It's important to read widely, but how do you know if a book is really worth your time? Just because something is in print doesn't mean it's hard-and-fast truth or that we should implicitly trust the author. For this reason, it's a good idea to learn how to evaluate your reading material. The following is an exercise I've done with both high school and college students to build discernment. It's designed for books, but you could apply this equally well to websites and online courses. Eventually, you'll be able to do this quickly, and for much of what you read. For this first time, though, take your time and try to answer each question thoroughly.

Begin by choosing a book you're interested in. It could be one you've already started, or one that's been sitting on your shelf for a while. Skim or read as much as you need to in order to answer the following:

1. Who is the author? Are they part of a specific tradition? Do they claim to have any notable degrees, initiations, or training credentials that uniquely qualify them to speak on the subject?

2. When was it written? What significant events or perspectives of the time may have influenced the writer?

3. Who published it? What other kinds of works do they publish?

4. What central arguments does the author make? What points are they trying to drive home to readers?

5. What peoples or groups are included in the book? Who is excluded?

6. Does the author use footnotes, endnotes, or some other citation style? What kinds of sources do they cite?

7. Is there a foreword or endorsement blurbs from other writers? Who?

Notice that I have not asked you to look at book reviews or other kinds of secondary commentary about the book. You may need to visit an author or publisher website to answer questions one, three, and seven, but by and large you should have a general idea about all of these from the book itself. It's great to get outside perspectives on books, but it's more important that you learn to evaluate things for yourself. None of the above questions should be thought of as dealbreakers, but they will give you a sense of where the book comes from, what agendas may be at work, and how many grains of salt you should take as you read it. All books have their failings, but likewise, a great many still have something to teach, even if it's what *not* to do. A book may be historically inaccurate but contain beautiful rituals or profound theological interpretations. Your personal brand of Witchcraft may be excluded, but perhaps others are detailed like nowhere else. You'll learn more when you stop looking for the perfect, single book, and you'll read more widely when you stop relying on others for guidance about what's good or not.

Fire

Books, of course, aren't the only way that people learn about Witchcraft. They may no longer even be how *most* of us learn much of what we know, since the internet and social media have become ubiquitous. In fact, many prominent, influential teachers and writers are *not* producing books. They share information through their online platforms, sometimes for free to drive traffic to paid online courses or spiritual services like divination or one-on-one mentoring. It makes some book-loving purists a little squeamish—admittedly, me too, on occasion—but overall this is good news for all of us, because it means that with a phone and a Wi-Fi connection, much of the world's knowledge is now available instantly and largely for free. Witchcraft is more accessible, and with greater variety, to more people than ever before. Are you taking full advantage of these resources?

Some of us avoid social media because we're concerned about consuming questionable information. A lot of us have been taught that books are always better (or in-person teaching is always better). Social media, we're often told, is toxic and superficial. Certainly that will be true if we only look at the worst of the internet, and if we don't flex those discernment powers on the regular. Most of the skills we use to assess books can be applied to blogs, websites, and social media posts, so be sure you're putting those to good use. When we do, we find that social media presents us with an extraordinary opportunity to learn, to be inspired, and to connect. For this quick and easy exercise, we're going to level up your internet experience.

Begin by flipping through your social media accounts. Perhaps you only have one or two, under your legal name. Perhaps you have a designated Witchy account. Or maybe you're like me, and you're basically everywhere. How does each platform make you feel? Why did you create your account to begin with? To connect with family? To find others like yourself? To collect funny memes? Social media platforms do not do all of these things equally well, so think about which you may want to overhaul for your magical purposes (or consider setting up an account on a new platform). You may want to create a separate, private account if you don't want Aunt Tilly to know you're a Witch (or not—Aunt Tilly might be into it).

First, search for the top Witchcraft accounts on the platform. Who are they? Who do they recommend? Who follows them? Be mindful that most social media accounts fall into two fundamental categories: info accounts run by someone purporting to be a teacher or other sort of educator and personal accounts detailing the thoughts and experiences of a single practitioner. The most informative accounts are often a mix of both. Remember, there's a lot to be learned by looking to the work of individuals just sharing their personal paths, so don't neglect these just because these users aren't setting themselves up as experts (and use your discernment skills to observe that not all "experts" are credible).

Follow the large accounts, but go out of your way to find less popular users and follow them too. If you're interested in a particular tradition, follow members of that tradition (use your hashtag skills and get creative). Go through their list of followers and find out who *they* follow, if that information is public. Fill your feed with Witchcraft, but do so critically.

As the days pass, notice which accounts are the most inspiring, and which lead to the most resources (book recommendations, other accounts to check out, tips and tricks that appeal to you and appear to be backed up by other practitioners). Unfollow the ones that don't improve your feed. Do not make the mistake of only following accounts that look like you or reflect your exact interests. Add practitioners of a variety of traditions, even those you aren't sure you agree with. Add people who challenge you to think more deeply, or who challenge your assumptions. White practitioners, add accounts run by people of color. Witchcraft spaces tend to be dominated by white women; be sure you're seeking out Black practitioners, Asian practitioners, and Hispanic practitioners. Add queer and nonbinary voices to your feed too. Americans, go out of your way to add Witches from other countries—you'd be amazed at how different the same tradition looks with an ocean in the middle of it (I'm a Gardnerian—I can affirm this!).

With as much time as we all tend to spend on our phones, make sure yours is working for you. Make it magical!

Water

Water is about going deeper, and, friends, your practice is not going to deepen by staying buried in books or hanging out online. People who find themselves in this stage tend to look for projects, research-oriented tasks, and just more obscure, convoluted magical texts they can use to distract themselves further from the reality that they just aren't putting very much of that study to practical use. Knowledge for the sake of knowledge is a beautiful thing, to be sure, but if your goal is to take things to the next level as a Witch and you've found that your impulse is just to keep reading, signing up for correspondence courses, or collecting magical materials produced by other people online, then it's time to disrupt that pattern. You know who you are.

Your task is to take a sabbatical from study. For real. Set a time period for yourself of at least a month, and abstain from your magical bookshelves. Pick something you've always wanted to try and go do it, or focus on building a routine with your personal practice. When you engage with text, let it be in the form of your own ritual notes and reflections. Get off those discussion forums, which are full of other people who *also* aren't practicing as much as they're running their mouths. Talk to your own gods, spirits, and personal guides instead. The books and the internet will be there when you come back, and you will have a deeper appreciation for them.

Earth

One of the biggest challenges for covenleaders, teachers, and other kinds of community leaders is not falling prey to our own egos. At some point, every book starts to feel like a regurgitation of the same information, every class and workshop starts to feel the same, and we develop pat answers for the seekers and students who come to us for help. When allowed to sit in this state for too long, it's easy to reach the conclusion that we must know it all. From here, it's only a short jump to missing an idealized, lost past (back when everyone did the work, put in the time, took things seriously, and knew what from what) and bemoaning the next generation of Witches for their various failings.

This isn't about chronological age—it's about time in the Craft. I've only been around for a bit over two decades, and I've found myself doing this too. For me, that idealized past is located back before social media, when people had to read books and do their own research (gosh darn it). For the generation before me, it was back when publishing was more exclusive and more people were working in covens, directly with teachers. And so on.

One of the symptoms of this sort of thinking is that we refuse to recommend or assign books that were published after our own training. Nothing beats the classics, right? When seekers and other sorts of newcomers struggle with these books (or object to their dated language, their treatment of sex, gender, race, or other social concerns), we let the fault lie with the seeker. We managed—why can't they?

Don't get me wrong—there are texts out there that I believe Witches of all kinds should absolutely engage with, despite their age. Just because people write new things doesn't mean we should wantonly discard the old. But ignoring current trends, current literature, and current concerns doesn't just do students and seekers a disservice; it also shortchanges us as Witches with living practices.

Choose a beginner book that was written in the last five years and work through it with beginner's mind. That means doing any exercises it contains too. It can be on any kind of Witchcraft you like, but try to choose one that is circulating heavily on social media and seems to be frequently recommended to newcomers today. Choose a book by an author you don't already know and maybe one who's only recently started publishing! When you find things you don't like or don't agree with, reflect on why, being as specific as possible. Journal your reactions, and note when you find things that might be beneficial for your own students, or even for yourself. I learn a lot by reading books for beginners, especially as those authors now tend to be younger than myself and have different backgrounds. It keeps my ego in check and helps me make better sense of some of the trends I notice in the broader community. I confess that sometimes I feel a little threatened, when things that I think are essential aren't included or when I feel my own tradition is being misunderstood.

But examining the part of myself that feels threatened almost always leads to new insights about myself.

Witchcraft is alive. It moves with the people who practice it, and sometimes the most striking insights come from people who are very different from ourselves. It is possible to engage with them without being disloyal to your own traditions—it might even grant you greater conviction. At best, you learn something new. At worst, you feel even more strongly about your personal Craft. You can't lose.

Chapter 7

Community

One of the very first spells I ever did was a petition spell that I hoped would help me to find other Witches. It was a pretty elaborate spell for a freshly minted teen Witch. I carved my name into a specially anointed candle, wrote out a detailed description of my request, and even drew a picture of myself, surrounded by friends. I still have the picture, tucked away in my first book of shadows. There I am, reading a book, sitting next to two other imaginary girls doing the same. The covers say *Wicca* and *Magick*, and we all look happily immersed in our studies. I wasn't looking for a coven at that point—just a group of friends I could share with and learn from. In retrospect, one of the reasons my spell didn't work was probably because I got *too* specific about it. I should've left things a bit more open-ended—my drawing was the limiting factor, detailing hair and eye color and probably impacting the likelihood of getting the results I wanted. Lesson learned! But looking back at it now, I was earnestly expressing a need that, for most of us, is one of the most basic.

As you know, Witchcraft is a path that, at its core, requires us to walk alone. You will have divine and magical experiences that will move you in profoundly personal ways and be impossible to explain to others, even those closest to you. You will wrestle with your own shadows, meet your own spirits, guardians, and gods. Your Will is your own, make no mistake, but that doesn't mean that all your magical endeavors have to be undertaken without friends, teachers, peers, and family. Just by virtue of being human, we are all part of an interconnected web. To some degree, we need others for comfort, support, and guidance and also to challenge us and keep us from stagnating. Being a part of a Witchcraft community can be instrumental in deepening your practice of the Craft. Plus it's also just a lot of fun, provided that community is both healthy and aligned with your personal goals.

In this chapter, we'll consider the interplay between practicing as a solitary Witch and participating in community, which is a lot more complex than beginner books make it seem. We'll also discuss the many types of communities that are now available, from formal covens to loose internet platforms, each of which have their perks and drawbacks. Newcomers, as well as the reluctant, will be encouraged to get out there and make contact as well as prepared to handle whatever awaits, both good and bad. For more experienced and, dare I say, curmudgeonly Witches, we'll reevaluate the role community plays in our practice and hopefully find new ways to engage, both as leaders and as casual participants.

Either-Or

No matter how hard we try to shake them, Witches seem to be all about dualism and dichotomies. How many times have you been asked if you're solitary or in a coven? If you're an introvert or an extrovert? A homebody or a social butterfly? These distinctions are almost never the whole picture, and most of the time they're not even very helpful. Most of us are both, or somewhere in between, or one way when we're young but different when we're older, depending on what day of the week it is. As Witches, especially as new Witches, we're often led to believe that we need to decide right away what sort of position, if any, we want to hold in the wider world of the Craft. Are you going to practice alone, or will you look for a coven?

There are two things wrong with this question. First, Witches in covens also practice alone. Most of your days aren't spent with your coven, after all, so if you're waiting around and not working magic, building relationships with your gods and spirits, nor delving into your own depths in pursuit of truth and personal power, then you're seriously missing out. A solitary practice is essential, no matter your tradition. Second, and most importantly, there are a ton of other kinds of Witch communities you could get involved in! Covens are only one type. They tend to be small, intimate, and structured in some way. In traditional Wicca and some other types of lineaged Witchcraft, they are usually hierarchical and exclusive. Eclectic covens may be much less so, but even these tend to be close-knit and have some kind of screening process for potential members. If coven life doesn't appeal to you (and it's definitely not for everyone), that's fine! That doesn't mean you're doomed to never have fruitful communal experiences. We all need to ditch the mentality that it's one or the other.

Why Community?

Most of the reasons to get involved with other Witches are pretty obvious: friends, fun, support, and all of that. Living as a Witch can make you feel like you're totally alone and misunderstood, and not in the mystical Witch-in-the-woods way. Aside from avoiding the crappy feeling of being stranded among people who won't understand you, it's enormously beneficial to have other people you can reach out to who live and think similarly and who can validate your feelings and experiences. But there are several less-obvious reasons to participate in some kind of community, some of which have as much to do with your magical development as they do your social life.

In intimate, training-oriented group environments, like those found in traditional Wicca and other styles of initiatory Witchcraft, members have the opportunity to share their magical experiences and receive feedback, either in the form of constructive critique or validation. Other, less exclusive types of communities can provide this as well. As long as you feel comfortable sharing -be it with an online community or a casual in-person meet-up—other Witches are usually quick to offer their own opinions about whatever you're up to. This could include anything from thoughts on why your spell didn't work, to other ritual techniques you might want to try, to whether the experiences you're having with a particular deity are typical or perhaps indicative of something else. Other practitioners will also point you to resources—books, websites, events, and lots more besides—that you might never find on your own. Even when you're all referencing the same texts and ideas, you'll find that everyone has a slightly different take on the matter and even casual discussion will bring to light perspectives that never occurred to you. If you approach a social situation with that beginner's mind we discussed in chapter 6, you'll find that, even when you're the most experienced person in the room, there will still be things to learn. Sure, you can accomplish some of the same things by reading widely, but listening to other Witches in discussion is often faster and more likely to yield surprises and new trails to follow. Plus, books can't offer you feedback on your specific circumstances.

Participating in community also keeps your Witchcraft grounded in the world. So much of ritual magic is about traversing in other realms, moving outside the physical body, and contacting non-human entities. People who live in these otherworldly spaces sometimes have difficulty functioning in the rest of their lives. That may or may not matter, according to your personal Will and aspirations, but if you're like most people, you have rent to pay, people who count on you to be present, and mundane goals and tasks that require your steady attention. Even if you're not worried about floating away on some astral plane, so to speak, it's easy to get out of balance. Some people end up becoming hyperfocused on making absolutely everything into something of magical significance without any discernment. This can look like seeing omens where there aren't any, forcing yourself to stay in toxic environments because you think you're supposed to learn some karmic lesson, or developing the hubris to think that the gods are speaking every time you have some impulsive thought, just to list some not-uncommon occurrences. On the flip side, some people allow themselves to be so consumed by the stresses of daily living that they lose touch with the Craft entirely. Other people can help you navigate this balancing act. Even if you choose not to share the intimate details of your life, just observing how other practitioners integrate the Craft into their lives will offer you consolation, inspiration, and encouragement.

Other Witches will also inevitably challenge you, whether or not they mean to. As much as we may wish to avoid conflict, it eventually finds us. Sometimes getting uncomfortable—because someone challenges our assumptions, offends our sensibilities, or calls our choices into question—is exactly the thing that kick-starts a new stage in our practice. The more you can expose yourself to other voices, especially marginalized voices that too often don't make their way into books and aren't widely circulated, the more robust your Witchcraft will be. There are things we learn by spending time with others that we can't learn alone, or at least can't learn as easily.

For teachers and group leaders, it's also important to have a sense of what's going on in the wider community, be it local, online, or otherwise. It's easy to get comfortable in our own covens, our own traditions, and our own networks and miss the changes that are taking place in our movements as a whole. Beware of living in an echo chamber. If your goal is to preserve your traditions and pass them to new generations, you need to know who those new generations are, how they speak and think, and what they value, not because you necessarily have to cater to them or change to appeal to them, but so you'll be able to communicate with them and make thoughtful choices in response to change. It's practically impossible to reach people—to teach, to serve—if you don't first try to know them. This doesn't mean you have to immerse yourself in public communities; it could be as simple as joining a new social media platform.

Ultimately, participating in community creates more learning opportunities than keeping entirely to ourselves. Lots of great ideas never make their way into books or blogs because they aren't deemed marketable or palatable enough, or simply because the people who have them aren't writers or well-known public figures. Other Witches can push our practices forward, faster. That doesn't mean you have to give up any of your autonomy or volunteer to start hosting Pagan Pride Day in your backyard. You might simply join a casual local meetup once a month or start hanging out in a new online group or forum where people share their experiences, whether or not you participate directly. Community can be as involved as you like, but it's worth getting out there one way or another.

Taking the First Steps

Where and how you look for community will depend on your specific goals and desires (which you will be asked to reflect on in one of the exercises at the end of this chapter!). If you're looking for something casual and anonymous, it might just be a question of following key hashtags on your favorite social media platform (and every social media platform has Witches, even if you have to dig a bit for the kind you're looking for). As you're comfortable, you may start making your own posts with those tags, liking or commenting on other people's posts, and allowing those relationships to develop over time. I can remember first getting the internet as a kid and being told to be cautious online because people would lie about their identities. For years after that lots of people would insist that online friendships weren't as meaningful as offline, and things like online dating and online religion were big jokes—the realm of people too socially awkward for real life. Now we know better. The internet is a part of daily life for so many of us, and it may be your best asset for meeting other Witches, especially if you're somewhat isolated. Some of my longest-standing Pagan and Witch friends are people that I met on YouTube. We find each other on other platforms as new ones come and go, and we share our lives over the years. Some I've been able to meet offline, but others I never have. Those relationships are no less real or important because they were forged online. And in the wake of the COVID-19 pandemic, even more communities have made their way online, even where people thought it wouldn't be possible. Festivals, conferences, rituals, workshops, and performances can all take place through the internet, and the quality of these is sure to improve over time.

This is a great place to start if you're either stepping out into the Witch world for the first time or just looking to explore something beyond what you already have. You'll find that each platform appeals to a slightly different demographic and has its own character, expectations, lingo, and taboos. Start with the one that's most familiar or most appealing. If you want to protect your privacy, consider creating a separate account. Then dive in and explore!

In-person communities can be trickier to find, but it gets easier every year as more and more people begin to explore magical paths and feel comfortable doing so with relative openness. Here, too, you'll probably start online. Use social media or a search engine to search "Witchcraft" or "Pagan" or "occult" plus the name of your closest big city, your state, or even your country depending on how big it is and how feasible travel is. Start narrow and then get broader. You may be looking specifically for traditional Witches, and all you can turn up are Wiccan groups, Pagan meetups, or socials for New Age practitioners, paranormal investigators, or tarot readers. That doesn't mean you won't find traditional Witches in these spaces—it just means that the organizers aren't highlighting them. I cannot stress this enough: *go anyway*. Even if it isn't quite up your alley. Most towns don't have an infinite number of options, so magically inclined people will tend to congregate where they can, even if their practices differ wildly. If you dig around and can only find a Unitarian Universalist church offering weekend meditation clinics or a health food store offering a class in herbalism, *go*. It might be a bust, but you could also find other Witches—maybe even some just like you—doing the same thing, just hoping that someone like *you* will show up. There is lots of Witchcraft crossover in New Age and tarot communities, geek and fandom communities, paranormal communities, kink communities, historical European martial arts communities, and environmentalist, feminist, and vegan/vegetarian communities. Treat it like a treasure hunt and go find your people!

Once you're ready to make contact, either online or in meatspace, the rules of other types of social engagements all still apply. You'll want to use good manners and be friendly, while still maintaining good boundaries and keeping your personal safety in mind, just as you would any time you meet strangers. It's tempting to think that Witch and Pagan communities will be inherently safer and more accepting, but I'm afraid this just isn't always true. People are people no matter their spiritual or magical persuasions, and we get predators and creepers just like every other community. So use your best judgment here.

If you're nervous about being awkward or saying or doing something alienating, it's okay to just sit back and listen to other people's conversations. You may or may not make tons of friends the very first time you go to a public event or a meetup, so it's okay to ease into it. Just remember to be honest and to be yourself! Sometimes newcomers feel like they need to show off tons of knowledge or experience to be welcomed, but that just isn't the case. In fact, I'd recommend not gushing about your credentials—if you have any—be that lineage, initiations, past leadership roles, or unusual magical abilities or proficiencies. Oversharing or appearing like a showboat or a know-it-all—even if you're not exaggerating in the least (though, let's be real, you probably are)—is less likely to impress and more likely to make others feel disinclined to share with you.

Above all, don't give up! You are bound to have at least a few not-awesome experiences out in the wider community. Just like in romantic relationships, most all of us kiss a few frogs along the way to finding our best partners. You'll meet people who rub you the wrong way. You'll sit through conversations and rituals that will bore you to tears. You'll go to events looking for like minds and there just won't be any. Keep going. Allow for the possibility every single time that you will be surprised. It's worth it.

Warning Signs

It's tempting to think that Witchcraft communities would be immune to some of the problems that occur in mundane spaces, but be aware that this is not at all the case. All the commonsense safety precautions that you use in other parts of your social life apply here too. Sometimes it can even be a bit trickier, especially for newcomers, because there are matters of magical etiquette and other community-specific pitfalls that you may have never encountered before. You might already know a thing or two about avoiding trouble at a bar or party, or how to recognize a sketchy situation at work or school or a bad romantic prospect, but what about an unhealthy coven or an abusive magical teacher? How can you identify red flags before getting in too deep with a group that could be detrimental to your practice?

Lots of the same warnings you might use in other potential relationships apply. Are they kind? Do they only talk about themselves? Do they make unwelcome sexual advances? Does your gut tell you to run? On top of the standard questions you can ask yourself, here are a few more indicators that you may be in for trouble down the road:

1. They Aren't Upfront about Their Tradition, Their Credentials, Their Affiliations, or Their Group Structures

Lots of groups are secretive, especially initiatory groups, but any potential coven or teacher should be transparent about who they are and what they're qualified to offer. The sorry truth is that sometimes people lie about their own training in order to convince others that they're authorities. If someone tells you they won't disclose their tradition, the identity of their own teachers, the source of their training, or how the group operates until after you've sworn an oath, look elsewhere. The inner workings of my intimate coven and the content of our book of shadows is oathbound, but the fact that we're Gardnerians is not. A potential student can use that information to scope out my group locally, ask other Gardnerians they may encounter if they can vouch for us (there are social media groups designed exactly for this), and then make an informed choice. That's perfectly expected and respectable behavior. There's a huge difference between protecting the privacy of a group and purposefully deceiving or misleading a seeker. If a potential teacher won't give you basic information that you can verify, that's a huge red flag.

2. They Do a Lot of Trash Talking about Other Groups, Traditions, or Individuals

Everyone has bad days, and not everyone has to like everyone else, but if you find that whomever you're spending time with can't get along with anyone else in the community, only has mean things to say about other Witches, and spends a lot of time gossiping about other groups, approach with caution. This often points to deep emotional baggage, a failure to resolve personal issues rooted in the past, and a lack of focus on their own personal spiritual development. Why dwell on other people when you could be doing Witchcraft?

3. They Use Shame, Name-Calling, Threats, or Yelling to Control Other People's Behavior

None of these things is ever acceptable, ever. Not in romantic relationships, not at work, not directed at children, and not in magical groups. Do not tolerate these from anyone, no matter how authoritative they seem, how much other people seem to like them, or how nice they were to you yesterday. It horrifies me deeply that I feel the need to include this, but I've seen more than one high muckety-whatever scream at their student or resort to name-calling when angry. Leave immediately, and do so the very first time it happens. Apologies are meaningless when no measure has been taken to address the bad behavior by the person committing it. Trust me on this one.

4. They Seem Overeager to Share Intimate Knowledge and Don't Respect Your Boundaries

Bringing someone into any kind of magical group is a big step for everyone involved, so most leaders will take it slow. You're likely to be asked to respond to an initial questionnaire, to hang out casually in a public setting over a period of time, and to receive acceptance and sensitive materials very gradually. Some groups are more cautious than others—and a totally open group may feel it has little to lose including you right away—but generally take it as a warning if things feel like they're moving too fast and you're uncomfortable about that. Be especially cautious if you're being pushed into sensitive situations, like skyclad ritual, initiatory experiences, or late nights in the homes of people you don't really know. Sometimes questionable teachers "collect" students and group members because they feel it gives them clout.

5. They Pressure You for Sex

Sex and sexuality are important in many traditions of Witchcraft (though not all, as is sometimes touted—my own coven includes asexual members, and their experiences are every bit as powerful and valid). However, no one should ever be pressuring you, especially a teacher. There is an inherent power differential between teacher and student, so consent is necessarily a problem. You also do not need to have sex with anyone to be initiated as a Witch. Sexual initiation rituals absolutely exist in certain traditions, but these lie in the realm of experienced practitioners prepared to engage with full knowledge and control of their choices. You should never be ambushed, forced, or otherwise coerced. If you are, get out.

6. They Require Payment but Discourage You from Asking for Testimonials or Seeking Out Reviews

There are perfectly reputable teachers and traditions that charge for their teachings or for membership. I've enrolled in several classes, long-term training programs, and weekend workshops myself over the years. But be wary if you are discouraged from consulting others about their experiences with the program or group. Look for reviews, ask current students about their opinions, and only sign up for courses that you feel good about paying for *and* can afford (going into debt is not required for learning Witchcraft and is surely a bad move). As an additional caveat, be aware that though other types of Witches may charge for membership in a coven or for initiation, traditional Wiccans do not. If you're pursuing Wicca specifically and someone hands you an invoice to become an initiate, proceed with caution.

7. Their Mundane Lives Are a Disaster and That Spills into Yours

Life gets hard for everyone at times, and no one is perfect. This is not a character flaw or a moral judgment—it's just true. I can tell you horror stories about low periods of my own and how they impacted the people I care about. It's not pretty. But as a seeker, you don't want to find yourself in a position where you're being asked to take care of someone else or sacrifice your own magical education for someone else's problems. When personal mayhem demands a leader's time and attention, the best choice for them is sometimes to put the group on hiatus or to pass leadership temporarily to someone else. What they definitely *shouldn't* do is pour their struggles onto their students indiscriminately, especially students who are relatively new or inexperienced. You can have compassion for someone and be supportive in their time of need without taking on their suffering.

I've met a lot of Witches over the course of my life and worked in a number of different group settings. Most people—*overwhelmingly*—are fundamentally good and wish you no ill, but each of the above has been a part of my own personal experiences out in the wider community. Abuse happens, and dysfunction exists, but they are usually recognizable so long as you're paying attention and don't allow yourself to be dazzled by the sheer newness of the experience and the desire to fit in as soon as possible. Remember always that you are an adult and can draw your own boundaries, no matter how new to Witchcraft you may be. Trust your gut, and have the patience to wait for other opportunities if the one at hand feels wrong for any reason. It's worth it to wait. Trust me on this one too.

Or Just Build It Yourself!

Even though Witchcraft has become more popular and Paganism more socially acceptable and common, your area may not have caught up yet. Sometimes as hard as we might look and as bad as we might want it, we just can't find our people. If that sounds like your situation, then it may be time to be the one to start something. Someone has to be the first, after all! Why not you? Maybe the prospect excites you, but if just the thought leaves you overcome with dread, take heed: you are in control, and you can be as big or as small about this as you want. You can also take things in stages. Maybe start with something small like setting up an online forum through your favorite social media platform. You could keep this online or ask people to meet up locally. My friend Venus began their community by inviting curious friends and acquaintances from a Pagan Pride celebration over for a Halloween circle. They wrote a simple ritual that took into account that their friends were new to anything like this and just framed it as a neat way to mark the holiday and share something important to them with friends. Their friends were into it, and when Venus held an Imbolc circle a few months later, they invited social media followers who lived locally. A year later, they have a thriving community of magically minded peers. Some are Witches, and others are merely curious, but it fuels Venus's practice either way.

If you don't want people in your home, consider meeting up at a coffee shop, public library, or park. You don't have to host a ritual. Instead, simply invite others to come and mingle, or perhaps start a book club or study group. If whatever you're planning requires more space or more privacy, consider renting something. Unitarian Universalist churches, yoga studios, community centers, and universities often provide event spaces for rent to the public. Restaurants and coffee shops sometimes do the same.

My first attempt at a Witchcraft group was a book club that met in the café of a big chain bookstore. I advertised with a flyer at the local metaphysical store and also at the local community college. That was before

Facebook (or even MySpace). Today, you could just post to social media. My friend Corvus rented space at a yoga studio when she decided to put together an open circle. She advertised online but also at the studio itself. And you know what? The first meeting, no one came! The next time, one person came! It took months, but eventually she had a small handful of regulars. Six years later, Corvus was running the city's only public Pagan group, with sabbat events that hosted as many as eighty people. It took a lot of patience, and your new group will likely require just as much. Don't be discouraged if your start is rocky.

If running a giant public sabbat like that sounds like a nightmare (it does to me), you could always start public and then close the group and make it private. Corvus herself eventually burned out a bit—that's a ton of work, and it was hard getting others to help out—but by then she had already met her closest friends, and eventually decided to pursue a small, initiatory coven with them. You're allowed to start something and then change course as your needs evolve. If you're a group leader or community organizer already and find yourself feeling run down or uninspired, consider that you may have outgrown your group! That's not a crime. We'll talk about what to do in that situation in the exercises at the end of this chapter.

Just as you should consider your motivation for finding community (more on that at the end of this chapter), it's even more important to consider your reasons for starting one. Reflect on the question. Do some journaling. Are you hoping just to make friends? Are you trying to build something where there isn't anything, or are you trying to create something different from what's already there? Is it your intention to attract more experienced Witches who might teach you? Or do you want to teach others? That last question is especially important. Whether or not we mean for it to happen, taking on the mantle of community organizer, moderator, or leader will make you an authority in the eyes of some of the people who will come through your doors. What it won't do is automatically make you *qualified* to teach, counsel, or speak for others. This can be a terrifying experience, but it can also lead to a swollen head and a hard ego trip. You don't need to be a self-deprecating altruist to run a group, but if you want to ensure it's healthy, fulfilling, and longstanding, you'll need to keep any grandiose ideas about your own importance in check.

Starting a group or a public event is an enormously rewarding experience, and you can do it no matter how experienced you are as a Witch, so long as you're upfront about what those experiences are. It's okay to be a beginner, and it's okay to be unsure of yourself! You just want to be honest about that with the people who come to you. Frame it as an opportunity to learn together. Organizing and maintaining any kind of group requires planning, dedication, and organizational skills, just as much as magical knowledge or experience. Actually, more so. Be creative, with the initial goal that you find just one other person. We often overlook the value of a magical twosome, but that's how plenty of covens start. Find that one other person—maybe they're already in your social circle—and take it from there.

The Life Cycle of a Group

Arguably the most influential coven—and certainly so among Wiccan Witches—is Bricket Wood, founded by Gerald Gardner in 1946 and home to a number of magical visionaries, authors, and household names, including Doreen Valiente, Jack Bracelin, and Fred Lamond. Bricket Wood remains active today.[26] That's incredible! That's more than seventy years—three quarters of a century. Longer than many of us can hope to live. Hardly anything we build lasts that long, especially in the United States. Pagan and Witchcraft groups tend to be especially short-lived, or so it seems. I've certainly seen plenty crumble over the years.

Why Bricket Wood should be spared, I can only guess, but I suspect that it might be misleading not to observe that both their leadership and membership has changed over the decades. No doubt their collective experiences, their ritual practices, their perspectives, their meeting times, and perhaps any number of other things has also changed, just given how much flux the world has seen since 1946. That's pure conjecture, mind, and from an outsider, but in my own years of coven leadership I've

---

26. "The History of Bricket Wood Coven," the Bricket Wood Coven, accessed April 16, 2021, https://www.bricketwoodcoven.co.uk/coven-history.

learned something essential: groups have cycles, the same way people and seasons do.

Groups—whether they are formal covens or public meetups—take on the character and the concerns of the people in them. As members learn and grow, so does the group as a whole. Groups can also have lulls, periods where they need to take breaks, reassess their practices and policies, or shift their collective focus, just like individual practitioners. A coven or an organization might retain its name over decades but functionally be quite a different group than when it first began. My coven, Foxfire, has had multiple incarnations as members have come and gone and as I've developed as a priestess.

Any group that you join or run is sure to do the same. Book clubs may slowly turn into ritual groups. Eclectic Witches discover that they'd like to explore a specific tradition together and begin becoming traditional. Staunch traditionalists cycle back to periods of exploration and eclecticism. Outer courts become inner courts. Festival boards split and form multiple events. Teen Witches grow up to be elders. Beginners turn into priests and leaders. To some extent, you can control change, but if you're practicing sincerely, you will grow. It's okay if that growth takes you in other directions. If you think of your group as a living entity, it will be easier to weather this change and to respond well to whatever cycles you notice. And, if you realize the group has run its course and it's time for you to move on, you'll be able to do so gracefully.

Dealing with Drama

A lot of people never get involved in Witch and Pagan communities because they don't want to deal with all of the drama that seems to go along with mixing yourself up in other people and their agendas. There are certain groups, public events, and big names who always seem to be at the center of things and carry particular reputations for pot-stirring and pettiness. There's something about people in large groups that seems to guarantee that, eventually, things will collapse, taking out every well-intentioned participant who makes the mistake of standing too close. Maybe it's just human nature. Add in the reality that Witches tend to be strong-willed, opinionated, and well-practiced in moving against the grain of wider expectations, and it's no wonder so many think getting wrapped up in a group or a social scene is just asking for trouble.

I've been an active participant in many magical communities over the years, in many cities, many traditions, and of many sizes. Some of my communities are online, as the internet makes it possible to connect no matter where we live. Every single one of them—from the most intimate closed coven to the biggest open community—has involved some drama from time to time. While at times frustrating and saddening, these kinds of interactions have also taught me a lot, not just about other people but also about my own needs, expectations, failings, and boundaries. Participating in the spiritual lives of other people provides opportunities for growth that really aren't available any other way. If you know how to survive, that is!

It's worth considering that a lot of what we write off as drama is really just people working through insecurities, fears, traumas, and embarrassments in public. If we like the people involved, the matter becomes a discussion, a rallying point, or a moment for collective support. If it's about people we disdain, however, we call it drama and try to sweep it into the trash heap. On some level, we're all wounded, and all of us have moments of weakness or points in our lives when we aren't at our best. Many who seem to thrive on community drama do so because it's entertaining. Being at the center of a drama, even if it's over something negative, means attention, which is something everyone needs from time to time. In the same way that a child might misbehave to get a parent to acknowledge them, an adult might spread a rumor, post an inflammatory comment online, or be obnoxious at an event in order to feel seen or important. Kindness garners fewer followers and shares than controversy, as I've learned in my own time online. It may sound trite, but I've found that the best way to deal with bad behavior is with compassion. When others are the cause, it's worth trying to empathize with their pain, whatever it is. Jealousy, insecurity, loneliness, anger, and boredom are often at the root, and these are things we all struggle with from time to time. Some of us were taught how to handle them in healthy ways, and some of us are still learning, but either way it's a work in progress.

I have also found that the drama in Witch communities is overblown. People are more likely to gossip, write blogs, and swap tales about negative things than about wholesome ones. It's easy to find yourself overexposed to the crappy stuff and to be left believing that that's all there is. Don't buy it. Witchcraft communities are full of smooth-running events, healthy covens, wonderful teachers, selfless leaders and organizers, intelligent discussion, and well-adjusted practitioners. Those things just aren't as sexy to talk about over drinks and are less likely to make it to the top of your social media feed.

Last, participating in drama is almost always optional. The situation may be different if we are being attacked directly, but rarely are the stakes so high. Most situations can be diffused by simply refusing to engage in them. Walk away. Unfollow. Block. Delete. Shift your focus. And where your engagement is required, as in matters of public safety, personal integrity, or in acting as an ally to the marginalized, arm yourself with honesty, directness, and composure.

• EXERCISE •
Building and Finding Community

With the exercises below, you'll be asked either to reach out and explore building community for yourself or else to reevaluate your place in the community you already have. Keep in mind that communities may be physical or online, small and intimate, or large and transient, and it is both acceptable and wise to choose to engage in ways that complement your personality and immediate needs. Challenge yourself—as always, I encourage getting uncomfortable—but respect your personal boundaries.

Air

Thanks to the internet and the growing number of Witches out in the world, you potentially have access to a wide variety of communities that you should explore, but the quality of your experience will depend largely on your goals. Take a moment to consider your purpose in seeking out a community. If you're already involved, and maybe feeling a bit weighed down by your interactions with other Witches, reflect on where your needs and desires lie in this moment. Get out a notebook and jot down your thoughts on the following:

1. What do you want from a community? What is it that you hope other Witches can offer you? Be as specific as you can here. If your answer is "I want to learn more," what specifically are you interested in learning? Describe your wish as completely as possible.

2. Are there other ways to achieve this? Other sources for meeting these same needs? What about being with others—whether in person or online—feels essential to you?

3. How large and how fluid would your ideal community be? Do you want something casual that allows for a certain degree of anonymity or something tight-knit and intimate?

4. How should authority and control function? Are you looking for something egalitarian or perhaps with some sort of governing body? A single leader responsible for guiding others? Perhaps you yourself aspire to leadership, and that is the root of your desire to find others.

5. This one is especially for those of you who've tried to get involved in community before and maybe been burned. What do you wish was different about the experience you had? Be as specific as you can. Would you change the people around you? The expectations? What do you think would deepen, revitalize, or inspire your relationships with your community?

Thoroughly contemplating the above can give you a better sense of yourself, before you throw other people into the mix. A lot of us find ourselves at times bemoaning Witchcraft communities for all number of failings, when really the problem is our expectations and the angle from which we're viewing them.

Fire

Many people practice for years and years before trying to make contact with other practitioners. Sometimes it's because they're nervous, or because they aren't convinced that community has anything to offer them. Sometimes it's just a matter of not knowing where to start! Hopefully, you've already picked up a few ideas in this chapter. In this quick exercise, you're going to take advantage of what's probably the fastest and easiest way to build connections with others—your phone!

Back when I was first exploring Witchcraft, the internet was a relatively new development. I taught myself how to use HTML and built myself a simple website. I also found my way into chat rooms and message boards, slowly making my way out of my shell and building connections with others. I didn't have access to an in-person community at that point, and the internet helped me to feel less alone. Nowadays, things are a lot easier (and you don't have to know any HTML). Getting in touch with other Witches and like-minded seekers and practitioners is a matter of getting on the right social media platforms, following the right hashtags, and having a little courage.

For this exercise, you're going to explore a new social media community. Pick your favorite platform or join a new one. If you need to, set up a second account just for your Witchcraft. And then join in. It's one thing to sign up and scroll through other peoples' posts, but challenge yourself to make your own. Comment on other accounts, share your thoughts, contribute your own posts, and say hello to strangers (exactly the opposite advice we were given in the eighties and nineties—strangers, it turns out, can be pretty awesome if you're careful about what you share and maintain your boundaries). If you're feeling particularly brave, consider video or photo formats, which can feel a bit more intimidating, but also humanize your interactions in a way that's hard to replicate with text alone.

Building community on social media can take a bit of time and effort, but keep at it. Make some kind of post every couple of days, explore new accounts, make friends, and allow yourself to follow the rabbit hole. We often speak of "the Witchcraft community" or "the Pagan community" as though it's a monolithic thing, but the reality is that there are many communities within these, and they don't always overlap as much as many of us like to think. Don't assume that because you didn't like one platform (or one in-person community, for that matter) that you won't like another. The people involved are often very different from one to the next! Explore and have some fun trying them all on.

Water

Okay, so you've been a participant in your local community for a while. Maybe you're a regular at a meetup, or even a member of a coven. Maybe you lurk at a lot of different types of events, keeping to the sidelines and just sort of soaking it in. It's one thing to participate in community, but it's quite another to be at the fore, facilitating that community for others. If you want to take community work deeper, it's important to explore taking on that role for yourself.

Your task is to stop *participating* in community and go *make* it. Earlier in this chapter I told you about my friend Venus, who used social media to start a ritual group that meets on the eight sabbats. They started out just by sharing their desire and asking if anyone local would be interested. They wrote a ritual (which would work even if no one else showed up), corralled a friend to help host (this also served to make sure that they would both be safe, as anytime you reach out to strangers it's important to make sure someone has your back), and then made the invitation open to people who messaged them to RSVP. People showed up! And it was a great time. A year later, they have a close group of magical friends who regularly do ritual together.

If that sounds a little too adventurous for your taste—Venus is one of the bravest people I know—you can start smaller. Maybe start your own online community (lots of platforms allow for the creation of pages, chats, blogs, and other ways to share), or ask a local leader you already have a relationship with to help you lead something for an established community. Lots of public Pagan and Witch clergy and facilitators are *thrilled* when someone else offers to take the reins for a night, especially if they know you're trying to get your feet wet as a ritual leader or teacher. Maybe approach a local bookstore and offer to run a free introduction to Witchcraft class, or lead a reading club with a magical focus. Even something small, like starting your own blog, will push you to relate differently to others in magical communities. Community isn't only about ritual groups or direct encounters with others—it's about building connections, and you can do that indirectly, through writing, sharing videos, and otherwise getting your thoughts out there. It's amazing who you can meet and how much you can learn, plus it's a surefire way to develop personal confidence and conviction.

You may ultimately decide that leadership isn't for you, and that's fine. Running any kind of group, public community, public forum, or event is a lot of work. Even if you discover you're really good at it, you may just not enjoy it, and that's as valid a reason as any to never do it again. But you will forever have the benefit of the experience! You'll appreciate the work that goes into creating community for others, and will have a greater sense of how to be the best sort of community member you can in the future. Of course, you could also find yourself with a new calling and allow your life to be transformed in ways you didn't anticipate. You never know.

Earth

It's really, *really* hard to be a community leader, whether you're the high priest of a coven, the president of a festival board, or the organizer of an open circle or teaching group. In other religious traditions, people who fill these roles are usually compensated somehow, but most Witchcraft and Pagan clergy and organizers do their work completely for free, and on top of working full time jobs and tending to their own families. It looks glamorous, especially if you're part of a tradition that has leadership positions that come with titles, special regalia, and lots of people deferring to you. But the novelty wears off quickly, and what's left is a lot of work, most of which goes on behind the scenes where no one appreciates it. Furthermore, when you're the one in charge of facilitating things for others, your own experience takes the backburner. You might host a beautiful, powerful ritual for the people in your group, but you're left feeling drained or spiritually unmoved. This is one of the many side effects of burnout.

One of the best ways to guard against burnout is to establish strong personal boundaries, both with yourself and with others. Most people won't deliberately take advantage of your time and energy, but both of those are required to function effectively in any leadership position. It's easy to fall into patterns where you're doing too much for people, saying yes when you should say no, eating into your own personal time, and crossing lines that you shouldn't in the quest to be helpful. Even people who love you will sometimes take as much as you're willing to give them, not realizing how it will run you down over time. This is one of the reasons why Witch and Pagan groups and community events don't last very long: leaders burn out, and no one wants to step into their shoes. But establishing boundaries can be tricky. It's a long process, and it will take time (it's also a great thing to discuss with a therapist or counselor, if you have access to one). At a particularly low point in my own coven leadership, I shared my struggle with boundaries with Angela Z, another high priestess and teacher in my tradition. Her advice was both extraordinarily simple and completely life-changing:

Make yourself a job description. When you start employment most places, you'll be given some kind of description of your role in the company. This document will detail your daily tasks, the expectations for your development long term, and who you report to (as well as who may be under you). You'll also have the opportunity to read job descriptions of other company roles, which are great for when you need to delegate a task to someone else or refer an inquiry to a more appropriate party. For this exercise, we're going to pretend your role as a community leader is like a traditional job.

You can do this as a series of short paragraphs or just a bulleted list. Describe your specific duties as completely as possible. Do you write rituals? Provide food? Handle funds? Teach incoming students (and if so, when and for how long)? Perform services like weddings or funerals (are you financially compensated for these, and if so, what are your rates)?

What are your hours? Are you on call, or do you have designated periods where you cannot be available? What credentials does your job require? My job as the high priestess of a coven, for example, does not include being a counselor or therapist. Not only does it not require those things, but I'm actually not qualified to fulfill that role, as I have no professional training as a therapist. Me trying to do the job of therapist on top of high priestess would not only lead to burnout, but it would also be misleading and potentially dangerous for my covenmates. Instead, I am prepared to refer covenmates to licensed therapists when they might benefit from those services. I'm also not a doctor, a parent, a maid, or any number of other things.

If you have a mundane job description you can look at, use it as a model. If you want to make things extra clear, draw up job descriptions for the other roles in your group. Provided your job descriptions are clear and thoughtful, you can even share them with the other members of the group (and ask them to write their own versions, coming to an agreement together).

When things come up that seem to cross into "not my job" territory, consult your own job description. Who *should* be handling it? How will you refer others to that person when the question arises (because it will)? Having a document in place will serve to remind you what is and isn't within your purview. You'll already know whether or not you should be saying yes to a new request, whether you're overstepping a boundary by taking someone's midnight phone calls, and what tasks you may be unintentionally neglecting in favor of others.

Chapter 8
Challenges

It's one thing to read books about how to be a Witch, but it's quite another to actually apply the principles and skills of Witchcraft to your life. We've spent a lot of time examining overarching ideas about numerous facets of Craft practice and philosophy as well as going over practical ways to live as a Witch, whether that means taking your first real steps into action or deepening what you've already built. I hope that you've moved through this text slowly and thoroughly, experimented with its contents, modified things to your liking, and followed many happy rabbit trails to other resources. It's time now to think about what comes next.

You could spend your whole life studying and practicing Witchcraft and still find yourself surprised. The process of integrating what you know (and what you're actively learning) into your life in a meaningful way takes time, experimentation, failure, and persistence. You'll find things that work for you and then grow to a point where they no longer serve. You'll develop as a person, learn new things about the world, and make different choices. Witchcraft is a constantly moving thing. If you try to pin it down and box it in, it will defy you. We've covered a lot of ground in the previous chapters, and soon we'll bring things to a close. Before we do, I'd like to touch on some of the trickier things that go along with being a Witch: figuring out who you are, practicing something that feels authentic to you, and working through hang-ups like imposter syndrome and the pressure that sometimes develops when Witchcraft feels like a contest with other practitioners. Witchcraft comes with challenges at every stage. It's likely that you've brushed against most of these at some point, and if you haven't yet, you surely will.

Living as a Witch

Living as a Witch is a process. There are turning points, certainly—moments when you feel like your identity is irrefutable, when power flows, and when your confidence is high—but a lot of your life is sure to be spent ebbing and flowing with whatever else is going on around you. Sometimes, you'll feel very Witchy, your energy levels will be high, and you'll be performing a lot of ritual, engaging with otherworlds on the regular, performing devotionals, and maintaining a personal practice that is daily. Sometimes, though, your family will have rough patches, your children or partners will need extra attention, your mundane job will feel out of control, you'll get sick, you'll struggle with community drama, or depression will strike. Sometimes it will be a struggle to engage with your Craft on a regular basis. That's just true.

Building strong foundations is the key to surviving low periods. If you have a strong sense of conviction and can articulate to yourself why it is that your work as a Witch matters, if you've built relationships within the Craft (be it with gods, spirits, or human communities), and if you have a regular practice made up of flexible, variable components that can shrink or swell with your needs, you will find that life's difficulties fit more easily into your Witchcraft. It will be harder to throw you off your game. I myself often fall back on prayer. In my tradition, the gods play a central role, and so communication with them keeps me afloat when I'm feeling unmoored. In yours, you may rely on a connection to a familiar spirit or your ancestors. You may find solace in your magical workings with plant and animal allies, in meditation and personal work, or in your occult studies. But find something. Lay strong foundations when life is smooth and you're feeling powerful. Take some time now to brainstorm some easy, quick things you'll be able to manage the next time you move through a low point. A one-line prayer, a charged candle you can light when in need of comfort, a favorite inspiring book close at hand with sticky notes at the good parts, a friend you can call who will encourage you. Anything you're confident you could pull off when you're not at your best. Lulls are normal, so plan for them.

When things are difficult and you can feel your power and interest waning, remind yourself that this is normal too. Don't beat yourself up for your humanity. Lots of Witches struggle with chronic illness, depression, and other clinical conditions that make daily tasks quite a bit more difficult than they are for others. Lots of Witches have children, spouses, parents, and loved ones who get sick, need support, and otherwise need our time and attention. Prioritizing their needs over your Craft doesn't make you a bad Witch. A good foundation in the Craft will help you to serve them—and yourself—better, but that probably won't look like tons of late-night coven meetings and long bouts spent alone casting spells. Being a Witch is also about how you think, how you react, and the choices you make.

Instead of berating yourself for a perceived failure, pay attention to your own natural cycles. When do you feel most like engaging consciously with the Craft? When do you struggle the most? Is this pattern seasonal? Lots of Witches find that they feel especially magical and excited about formal ritual and exploration right around Halloween. I find that I have the most energy in the spring and summer. If you menstruate or are conscious of other hormonal cycles, don't underestimate how much these can impact your mood! And if you struggle with clinical depression, ADHD, chronic illness, anxiety, or any other sort of condition that impacts your daily life, be as kind to yourself as you possibly can. When people say that Witchcraft should be challenging and get you comfortable with being uncomfortable, that's about pushing your magical boundaries and changing your thinking, not hurting yourself physically or emotionally. You're not doing it wrong just because you need to take breaks and tend to your personal needs. We all have to do that from time to time, though we don't usually advertise the fact on social media or at the local meetup. You might feel like other people have things more together than you do and live perfect lives, but I promise they don't.

You have your whole life to be a Witch. It doesn't matter if you feel like you're off to a late start or if you have bouts where you can't focus as well as you'd like. Let your path be a process and trust that each day carries you forward.

The Quest for Authenticity

What makes someone a real Witch? Being initiated into a particular tradition? Having a sincere heart? Being chosen by a god or spirit? Having "Witch blood" and coming from a magical family? The ability to work effective magic? Can you become a Witch, or do you have to somehow be born one or have latent powers? Is that even possible?

No matter how long you've been practicing Witchcraft, you've probably got your own answers to many of those questions. Maybe they're deeply held convictions based on tested experience, or maybe they're preconceptions based on what you've heard from others or read in books, but have you noticed how passionate people tend to be about their answers? Even though Witchcraft takes myriad forms and has many histories and traditions, we tend to be quick to draw lines between who's real and who's not, who's doing it right and who's only in it for the attention or because they like the spooky aesthetic.

Witchcraft is heavy and powerful. It changes lives and shapes worldviews, so it's perfectly natural that we would want to ensure that we were practicing well and fully. It's equally natural that we would want others to treat it with the respect and reverence that we do. *Authenticity* has become something of a buzzword, but it's one that resonates with a lot of us. We all want an authentic Witchcraft—a Witchcraft that is true to our ideals and expresses who we are, both as individual practitioners and as bearers of a tradition that has been passed in power across time. Witchcraft is too much work to be wasted on something that doesn't feel true and real.

No one else can give you the reassurance that your practice of the Craft is authentic. As you know by now, Witchcraft isn't a singular tradition with one history and one collective set of coherent beliefs and practices. Even those of us who belong to established traditions see a lot of differences between us. There is no singular authority who can tell you definitely that what you're doing is correct and meaningful. You have to feel that on your own. No matter what path you choose, you will read things and meet others that will tell you that you're not doing it right and you're not a real Witch. If you pay these voices too much mind, you will hobble your practice. Read widely, explore perspectives that differ from your own, and heed the advice of people you trust and respect. Be open to criticism but not bogged down by it. Most of all, reflect on your own feelings and experiences, pay attention to what works for you and what doesn't, and use your discernment and good judgment. The only truly authentic Witchcraft is the one that works.

Dealing with Imposter Syndrome

One of the biggest reasons why Witches are so invested in the pursuit of authenticity is that, deep down, too many of us are struggling with the anxiety of whether or not our own practice of Witchcraft is legitimate and real. Even before we start to analyze what it means for something to be "real" or what makes one sort of Witchcraft more legitimate than another, there is that deep, sinking feeling that many of us carry around that whispers, "You're making this up," or "You don't know what you're doing," or "Other people are living more magical, powerful lives than you." I'm convinced that the reason why some of us are so vehement about policing other peoples' practices, drawing lines between whose Witchcraft is more authentic than whose, and fighting about which traditions are older/darker/more powerful/more serious is because, secretly, people are worried that their Witchcraft isn't what it should be. Some of us respond to anxiety by attacking others—dismissing whole traditions, targeting individuals with accusations of insincerity or shallowness, or loudly proclaiming our innate magical specialness. Tearing other people down makes us look a little bit taller, and it's a lot easier than focusing on our own development. I've been guilty of this myself, and I've certainly been a target as well.

When you find yourself feeling dismissive or threatened by someone else, it's worth working out the reasons why. It's very likely that you're projecting your own frustrations, anger, and insecurity. It's important to remember that your focus should be *you*, and other people's magical lives are neither within your purview to change, nor do they have any real impact on you. It's okay not to agree with someone else's beliefs and traditions. It's okay for other Witches to do what fuels them.

But the other way that we can react to this anxiety is to internalize it, absorbing the message that we just aren't doing it right, are only pretending or playing at being a Witch, and that if everyone else doesn't already know, they will the second we open our mouths. This is called imposter syndrome, and it's a problem in pretty much every other area of life as well. Just check out any community of artists or writers! Is playing an instrument all it takes to earn the title "musician," or do you need to have a particular level of proficiency? Does writing a blog or scribbling poetry in a private notebook make you a "writer," or do you have to publish? Does self-publishing count? Are you only an "artist" when people are willing to pay for your work?

It's an awful feeling! It ruins careers, keeps people from pursuing their dreams, and triggers depression, among other things. And we do it as Witches too! We tell ourselves that we're lazy, that our magic doesn't really work, that we're not naturally good at things, and that other Witches are more powerful or more spiritual or more committed than we are. If only we were just better—if we were more talented, had the right training and initiations, had better tools, could build prettier altars, or could afford all the books we wanted.

The first step to defeating imposter syndrome is to understand that everyone struggles with it at some point. Beginner Witches, occult scholars, high priestesses, and Witch authors and teachers all struggle with insecurity from time to time (and sometimes more frequently than we want to admit). Seriously. When I first began exploring Witchcraft, I was practically obsessed with "doing it right." At first, I worried about my spells working, but it didn't take long before I learned to worry that I wasn't really a Witch because I wasn't in a coven and wasn't initiated. I had no Witches in my family, either, so no way to claim some fantastical birthright. Years later, once I *was* in a coven, I was taught to worry that it wasn't the right *kind* of coven. More years later came nasty debates about whether or not the Witchcraft I'd come to love—Wicca—was even really Witchcraft at all. With a history rooted in ceremonial magic and contemporary movements like New Thought and Theosophy, surely it wasn't as authentic as other kinds of Craft, which were supposedly unadulterated.

I've had more than two decades in Witchcraft at this point and it's never let up. It's so easy to find something to be insecure about, and—trust me—it only gets worse as you become active in public communities and start taking on leadership roles. There is no point at which you are suddenly granted confidence. No point at which everyone will acknowledge what you're practicing as correct and legitimate. You have to build that confidence yourself. That can be a long process, and it will have ups and downs, but there are several practical steps you can take now to combat magical insecurity where it occurs (especially now that you know you're not alone).

First, reflect regularly on where you started and how far you've come. This is my favorite use for my own magical records. Sometimes we're so busy faulting ourselves for our perceived failings that we lose sight of how much we've learned and where we've grown. Are you further along now than you were the last time you checked in with yourself? Then you're on the right track. Growth as a Witch doesn't really happen in a straight, upward slope, either. It zigzags! So don't dwell on the mistakes you make. Instead, look at larger patterns. What all have you learned? What new things have you tried? Where have you demonstrated more confidence, more maturity, more control? Celebrate those things, and do so often!

Second, focus on you. Make a point of not looking too hard at what other people are up to, be it on social media or in your own coven or tradition. Others can offer guidance and provide us with inspiration and feedback, but for the most part your attention needs to be on your own Craft. Envy and doubt can sneak in without our even realizing it, and too many people turn Witchcraft into a contest that nobody can win in the end. All any of us can do is the best we can, so stop comparing yourself to other Witches. In a similar vein, avoid drama and gossip where possible. Most of us, whether we like to admit it or not, enjoy a good community scandal periodically, but every moment you spend worrying about someone else is a moment you could be doing something to benefit yourself. Like practicing Witchcraft.

On a related note, don't do things that make you feel bad later. This was a lesson I learned in my twenties, when I was in therapy for the first time working my way through self-injury and a substance abuse problem. I've found it applies pretty well to managing imposter syndrome as a Witch too. Take a minute to think about when you struggle the most. Is it when you're comparing yourself to others? When you've overwhelmed yourself with new material you feel like you're supposed to master? When you've overcommitted to helping others? Work to be conscious of what makes you feel less-than and then...don't do those things. Maybe easier said than done (okay, definitely easier said than done), but shifting our awareness really can do wonders. Opt out of behaviors that inhibit your joy.

Finally, stay humble. There's nowhere to fall if you don't climb up on a pedestal to begin with. Remember that you're always a student—always learning and growing. No matter how many other Witches you may teach, perform ritual with, or befriend, and no matter if you're a coven elder, an author, or a community leader, if you think of yourself as a student first and admit openly what you don't know, you can't be an imposter.

Confidence comes in time, and even the most powerful Witches you know struggle with imposter syndrome. Allow yourself to feel how you feel in the moment, consider what's behind those feelings, and then keep going.

Being in Community

The idea of the Witch alone is something of a paradox. On the one hand, we are all walking our own paths, connecting directly with powers greater than ourselves (or harnessing those powers *within* ourselves), and are ultimately responsible for our choices and the fulfillment of our own divine Will. Even if you are in a coven, your Witchcraft is always your own. On the other hand, the very concept of the Witch is socially constructed. One cannot be an outsider unless there is something to be outside *of*. These boundaries are erected culturally, by people sharing experiences, agreeing upon language, and deciding collectively what lies inside and outside of those boundaries. Just by claiming the word *Witch*, you become part of something that is collective. Reading Witchcraft books, attending Witchcraft events, participating in Witchcraft spaces online—these are social acts, even if you do them from the privacy of your own home. You cannot help but be in conversation with others, responding to their ideas and building your own frameworks in relation to theirs, be it through the consumption of media or direct textual or verbal communication. No Witch is ever truly solitary, though we all walk the path alone. It's a tricky place to live.

No matter what your own Witchcraft communities look like or how deeply entwined you are within them, the actions and ideas of others in these communities have real impact on all of us. We are interconnected, whether we want to be or not. If you are open to them and everyone has healthy boundaries and mutual respect, these connections are truly one of the most joyful parts of practicing Witchcraft. I encourage you to embrace these where you can. Read widely, be social, go to public events when you can, make friends online, and withdraw into contemplative solitude when you require. As with all things, we move in cycles here.

At times, you might feel like Witchcraft is a competitive sport. So much of social media is about getting us to buy things, and even books become a contest between who has read more, who has access to the rarest titles, and who understands them best. Covenleaders who should know better mistake being prolific initiators for being effective leaders and teachers. Community organizers get big heads. We all get judgmental sometimes, but there's a way to be constructive about it. Judgment can serve us as we maintain our boundaries and practice discernment—you don't have to like everyone or be everyone's friend. It often comes as a shock to Witches, even experienced ones, that while Witchcraft may be inherently political, that doesn't mean our politics look the same. You will encounter prejudice. You will encounter other Witches who hold beliefs you find abhorrent.

As always, learn to centralize your own Craft, and use it to improve on the world where you can. Keep an open mind when you encounter disagreement, but be firm in your most deeply held convictions. Get good at saying no, and mean it when you say yes. Don't turn other Witches into your competition, whether you're fighting to feel heard, fighting to belong, or fighting for control. We always get farther when we work together.

• EXERCISE •
Prepping for the Future

I hope you're feeling encouraged and inspired, as we approach the end. There are some difficult issues in this chapter, and I hope you've encountered questions and ideas throughout this book that you'd like to pursue and develop once you finish reading. As we arrive at the final exercise, it's time to integrate our four elemental perspectives. This final task varies only according to your own creativity, proclivities, and desires. You may get as complex with it as you like, or keep it absolutely as simple as possible.

Practically everything about Witchcraft is related to cycles, from seasonal holidays, to many of our most dearly held myths, to the patterns apparent in our magic. Your explorations and moods are cyclical too. You will have points in your life when you are anxious to learn more and level up your practice, and you will experience lulls. Sometimes you'll need to coast for a while. Other times you'll hit walls and feel like all of the enchantment is hemorrhaging out of your life. It happens to all of us, and it's perfectly normal. It is my sincere hope that I've left you feeling energized and excited for what comes next, but you know the wheel is going to continue turning. Why not boost your intent right now and prepare for future lulls at the same time?

Begin by contemplating or journaling about the following:

1. What is the best thing about being a Witch?

2. What dreams do you have for yourself in your practice? What skills do you want to master? What do you want your practice to look like in ten years? Who would you love to meet? What magical places would you love to visit? What roles do you want to have in the community? Think of this as a wish list for your Witchcraft.

3. What positive things have come from your practicing the Craft?

4. How are you a better person for being a Witch?

5. Why is the world better with Witches in it?

6. What images, objects, books, and art get you the most excited about Witchcraft?

Get cheesy with all of these and go over the top. Gush. Be as honest and as thorough as you can. Get a big head. Be bold about what you want and what you love. This is just for you. Generate as many ideas as possible.

Next you're going to capture these feelings and save them for your future self, just in case they ever need a hand (spoiler: they will). Sometimes we need to be reminded of what matters to us, whether that's because life gets in the way, we lose focus, depression creeps in, or we just get so busy that we forget ourselves. There are always new walls to break though, so give yourself a hammer. Use the ideas you've come up with for the questions above to create a reminder for yourself. You can do so in the form of a letter directed at yourself to be opened at a low point or just when you need some additional encouragement. You can create a video of yourself sharing your thoughts, make a vision board or some other form of visual artwork that you know will inspire you, or write a poem or song. You can even create a care package. Fill it with all the things that inspire you: your letter to yourself, a candle or herbal blend you've created and charged for inspiration or encouragement, a favorite book that gets you excited, images of the things you still want to accomplish or places you want to visit, and anything else you can imagine. Think of it as an emotional emergency kit. Put it under your bed or in a closet, and forget about it. When you need it, it'll be there. It's a small thing, but your future self will appreciate it one day.

Conclusion

Throughout this book, I've gone to lengths to offer Witches of all persuasions insight and advice for where to go next—how to take your practice deeper and to expand beyond what you've already been doing. No matter what sort of Witches we are, we can all benefit from particular techniques and strategies that address how we learn, how we interact with others, and how we understand ourselves. Those things aren't tradition specific. No matter who you are as a Witch and what flavor of Craft you've chosen to explore and dedicate yourself to, there are practical steps you can take to push things to the next level.

There is a real clamor for advanced work in Witchcraft communities. In all of my time as a covenleader, as a teacher, and as a participant in magical spaces, this may be the complaint that I hear the most frequently. With all the people who have been attracted to Witchcraft and with the plethora of books available and growing every year, you'd think we would have collectively matured as a movement. You'd think those advanced materials would be easy to find. I hope I've persuaded you that there are, in fact, better resources, but the point still stands: our collective movement often lacks depth and meaning. Lots and lots of people come to Witchcraft, poke around for a few years (and often a lot less), and then move on. I can name too many elders and teachers active for a time and then leaving, not just their public communities but their traditions as a whole.

There's only so much we can control as individual Witches. The character of your local community and the books available for sale at your local bookstore may be outside your influence, but your personal approach to Witchcraft is not. And for many people, the lack of depth in their Witchcraft is due to their approach. Too many of us expect the power and meaning to just be handed to us or for sale down at the local metaphysical store.

It is popular right now—and has been for years, really—to insist that Witchcraft is whatever you need it to be. It's also increasingly popular to insist that it's only a craft, not a religion at all, but a skillset that anyone can learn and explore. I accept these positions to an extent and have acknowledged them throughout this book.

But if we treat Witchcraft only as a tool that we can pick up and put down at will, is it any wonder that it lacks depth and meaning? There are many definitions of the word *religion* and many ways to be a devotee of any singular tradition, but many of us discount these things entirely because we don't want to draw parallels with religious movements and communities that have wounded us. *Religion* makes us recoil. This might be understandable. As Witches, we are invested in our sovereignty, our autonomy, our personal power. Even those of us who believe in gods often balk at words like *worship* and *service*. We might even avoid communities because we worry that others will infringe on our control over our own practices.

But as long as your Witchcraft is only about yourself, or only about using magic to manipulate the world to be better only for you, it will be lacking. Eventually you will hit a bottom—an inescapable plateau—and might conclude that it is the Craft itself that is the problem.

You don't have to call your practice religion, and you don't have to worship gods, but when you encounter people who have been truly transformed by Witchcraft on a deep level, who have taken their work a place even further, consider how their approach might differ from yours. For most, that approach has been one of devotion, of priesthood, of centering their Craft outside of themselves, perhaps in service to a community, to an ideal, or to a higher power. Each can refuel and offer meaning and support that is difficult, if not impossible, to achieve alone.

No one will hand meaning to you. It's easy to dabble in Witchcraft, and it certainly *is* available to everyone. But the decision to go deeper is on *you*. I hope that you will.

Though I could never cover everything—no book is ever complete—I hope I've given you a lot to ponder and experiment with here. More often than not, taking the next step in your Craft and kicking things up a level has very little to do with acquiring difficult, convoluted knowledge or gaining admission into secretive groups or exclusive schools and orders (not a bad strategy, but we have to take seriously that this just isn't an option available to everyone or even *appropriate* for everyone). It's not even necessarily about doing *more* as a Witch. Instead, it's about rethinking your approach, reevaluating what you're *already* doing, and trying things again with a fresh perspective. And—most importantly—being brave enough to change your mind, to play, to not fit in, and to carry on when things are difficult.

Give yourself the time to process these exercises and concepts. Revisit them in a year or so and see if anything has changed for you. Read authors who disagree with me or whom you disagree with yourself. Take opportunities that arise to learn more, but also create them. Value yourself and the work you put in, and be honest about your goals and intentions. Don't be afraid to explore another tradition, to ask difficult questions, or to be the person in the room who says, "No, I'd rather do it another way."

I'm sure, down the road, I'll look back on some of what I've written here and I'll wish I'd rephrased things or shared something different altogether. Witchcraft is an enormous subject, especially if we're speaking broadly and trying to go deep. The most astounding thing to me about being a Witch is that I'm always changing, growing, learning new ways to do things, and shifting my thinking about my tradition, my gods, my personal practice, my coven leadership, and my teaching. You will too, I have no doubt, no matter what your Witchcraft looks like right in this moment.

Witchcraft doesn't stand still. It doesn't petrify or stagnate. And if you practice it sincerely, it will change you in every way imaginable.

Bibliography

Berger, Helen A. *Solitary Pagans: Contemporary Witches, Wiccans, and Others Who Practice Alone*. Columbia: University of South Carolina Press, 2019.

Clarke, J. J. *The Tao of the West: Western Transformations of Taoist Thought*. New York: Routledge, 2000.

Crowley, Aleister. *Magick Without Tears*. Scottsdale, AZ: New Falcon Press, 1991.

———. *Magick: Liber ABA, Book 4*. York Beach, ME: Samuel Weiser, 1997.

———. *The Revival of Magick and Other Essays*. Edited by Hymenaeus Beta and Richard Kaczynski. Scottsdale, AZ: New Falcon Press, 1998.

Cunningham, Scott. *Wicca: A Guide for the Solitary Practitioner*. St. Paul: Llewellyn Publications, 1994.

Dunlosky, John, Katherine A. Rawson, Elizabeth J. Marsh, Mitchell J. Nathan, and Daniel T. Willingham. "Improving Students' Learning with Effective Learning Techniques: Promising Directions from Cognitive and Educational Psychology." *Psychological Science in the Public Interest* 14, no. 1 (2013): 4–58. doi:10.1177/1529100612453266.

Eliade, Mircea. *The Sacred and the Profane: The Nature of Religion*. Orlando, FL: Harcourt, 1957.

Fortune, Dion. "The Rationale of Magic." *London Forum* 60 (1934): 175–81.

Frost, Robert. *A Witness Tree*. New York: Henry Holt and Company, 1942.

"The History of Bricket Wood Coven." The Bricket Wood Coven. Accessed April 16, 2021. https://www.bricketwoodcoven.co.uk /coven-history.

Leach, Evan A., Helen A. Berger, and Leigh S. Shaffer. *Voices from the Pagan Census: A National Survey of Witches and Neo-Pagans in the United States.* Columbia: University of South Carolina Press, 2003.

Lévi, Éliphas. *Transcendental Magic: Its Doctrine and Ritual.* Translated by Arthur Edward Waite. London: Bracken Books, 1995.

Maslow, Abraham. *Motivation and Personality.* 2nd ed. New York: Harper & Row, 1970.

Murray, Margaret. *The God of the Witches.* New York: Oxford University Press, 1952.

Penczak, Christopher. *The Inner Temple of Witchcraft: Magick, Meditation, and Psychic Development.* St. Paul, MN: Llewellyn Publications, 2002.

Pratchett, Terry. *Wintersmith.* New York: HarperCollins Publishers, 2006.

Regardie, Israel. *The Golden Dawn: The Original Account of the Teachings, Rites, and Ceremonies of the Hermetic Order.* Edited by John Michael Greer. Woodbury, MN: Llewellyn Publications, 2018.

Roach, Marilynne. *The Salem Witch Trials: A Day-by-Day Chronicle of a Community Under Siege.* Lanham, MD: Taylor Trade Publishing, 2004.

Three Initiates. *The Kybalion: Centenary Edition.* New York: TarcherPerigee, 2018.

Further Reading

As you take the next steps in your personal practice of Witchcraft, the following books may provide much needed guidance in the form of history, further advice on specialized subjects, strategies and perspectives in teaching and leadership, and additional context for placing Witchcraft within the wider landscape of religion and magic as a whole. Some of these are academic treatments, written by trained scholars of history, religious studies, and neighboring disciplines. Others are by practitioners—Craft leaders and teachers, theologians, and researchers. Some of these will have more appeal to beginners or intermediate Witches, while others are most applicable to group leaders. I encourage you to read widely, accept the challenge of books that might seem outwardly intimidating, and have fun pushing yourself with texts outside of the Witchcraft genre.

Albanese, Catherine L. *Nature Religion in America: From the Algonkian Indians to the New Age*. Chicago, IL: University of Chicago Press, 1990.
Something of a classic in the field of American religious studies, this is a study of "nature religion" in American history. Pagans and Witches are prone to describing their traditions as "nature-based" or "nature religions," but what does that actually mean? Where do these beliefs come from, and are they unique to us? This book also serves as a useful crash course in the histories of some of Witchcraft's biggest (and often unsung) influences: New Thought and Transcendentalism.

Boyer, Pascal. *Religion Explained: The Evolutionary Origins of Religious Thought.* **New York: Basic Books, 2001.**

Why do we have religion? Why, despite the advancement of science and the supposed disenchantment of the world, does religion persist? Psychologist and anthropologist Pascal Boyer proposes evolutionary explanations, and demonstrating that religion is, despite popular criticism, very reasonable! This book is very useful for Witches who wish to understand a bit more about magical thinking and how it shows up in our day to day.

Copenhaver, Brian P. *Hermetica: The Greek Corpus Hermeticum and the Latin Asclepius in a New English Translation with Notes and Introduction.* **New York: Cambridge University Press, 1992.**

In the present book, I've alluded to the impact of Hermeticism on Witchcraft, especially as it has been interpreted by New Thought and the popularly cited (and highly contested) work *The Kybalion* by Three Initiates. This is not even remotely a complete picture! The *Corpus Hermeticum* is a body of texts that have been informing Western magical traditions for centuries. For Witches who want more, Copenhaver gives us both an English translation and a thorough introduction.

Davies, Owen. *America Bewitched: The Story of Witchcraft After Salem.* **New York: Oxford University Press, 2013.**

America's relationship with Witches is complex. In this excellent, thorough history, longtime scholar of magic and the occult Owen Davies takes us on a tour of American Witchcraft since the Salem trials. Many of the most-often recommended histories deal with Britain, but American readers would do well to explore things a bit closer to home.

Denton, Melinda Lundquist, and Richard Flory. *Back-Pocket God: Religion and Spirituality in the Lives of Emerging Adults.* **New York: Oxford University Press, 2020.**

This one is for all us olds complaining about young Witches on social media. The religious landscape has changed so much for young people in recent decades, especially with the advent of the internet and the smartphone. How do young people today learn about religion and incorporate it into their lives (or not), and what are the consequences? Denton and Flory are sociologists, so this book is packed with interesting data. A useful book for covenleaders working with young adults or for anyone interested in the changing face of Witchcraft culture as the result of young people on the internet.

Drury, Nevill. *Stealing Fire from Heaven: The Rise of Modern Western Magic.* **New York: Oxford University Press, 2011.**

Any history of Witchcraft—regardless of tradition—would be incomplete without a thorough exploration of European esotericism as a whole. Our histories are intertwined with those of organizations like the Hermetic Order of the Golden Dawn, the Ordo Templi Orientis, and many others (some quite surprising). In this accessible survey, Drury introduces readers to these, as well as the colorful, fascinating figures captaining them. Not only will this provide insight into our practices as Witches, but it will also serve as an excellent starting point for Witches who find themselves interested in pursuing the occult more broadly.

Freedman, Harry. *Kabbalah: Secrecy, Scandal and the Soul.* **London: Bloomsbury Continuum, 2019.**

Qabalah (or Kabbalah or Cabalah, depending on your perspective) undergirds a number of traditions within Western esotericism, including Wicca and some other kinds of Witchcraft. It can be intimidating to learn, however, and, beyond that, is the subject of increasing controversy in magical communities. Freedman is a scholar of Judaism and holds a PhD in Aramaic. Here, he provides readers with a fascinating history of Kabbalah, including its appropriation by occultists. An excellent foundation for further studies, and with no scholarly background required.

Fuller, Robert C. *Spiritual but Not Religious: Understanding Unchurched America.* **New York: Oxford University Press, 2001.**

Though this is an older title by scholarly standards, the trends that Fuller details seem to me to be only more apparent. Are "spiritual" people necessarily up to something distinct from "religious" people? Why might someone choose one term over the other, and how did this trend develop? Fuller notes the patterns and proclivities of Americans (though I think Europeans will find these arguments applicable as well) who live outside organized religion. This is a helpful book for understanding many of the trends in Witchcraft and other magical communities. Our movements do not exist in a vacuum, and when we zoom out, we may be a little less outside the mainstream than we think we are.

hooks, bell. *Teaching to Transgress: Education as the Practice of Freedom.* **New York: Routledge, 1994.**

If you want to be a better teacher of Witchcraft, you cannot only study Witchcraft. You must study teaching. bell hooks (and, no, the lack of capitalization is not a typesetting mistake!) offers readers absolutely priceless analysis of how our classrooms are impacted by boundaries—of race, of class, of gender—that are too often invisible to people in positions of power and privilege. How can we build educational spaces that serve all students? You may not work in a classroom, but these problems also exist in our covens, groves, and circles. Few books have had as much impact on my own philosophy as a covenleader.

Knight, Shauna Aura, and Taylor Ellwood, eds. *Pagan Leadership Anthology: An Exploration of Leadership and Community in Paganism and Polytheism.* **Stafford, UK: Megalithica Books, 2016.**

This book promises to be particularly useful to group leaders and event organizers. Covering everything from building and maintaining good personal boundaries, dealing with communication issues, and responding to community predators, this collection of essays from a number of experienced leaders within a variety of traditions is indispensable, whether you're running a coven or dreaming of organizing a Pagan Pride event.

Lévi, Éliphas. *The Doctrine and Ritual of High Magic: A New Translation.* **Translated by John Michael Greer and Mark Anthony Mikituk. New York: TarcherPerigee, 2017.**

This work is a treasure trove of insight into the origins of a great deal of Witch philosophy, liturgy, and some of our most heavily circulating aphorisms. This is an especially important read for Wiccan Witches, as this is a direct ancestor of these traditions. Greer and Mikituk's translation is clear and readable, and Greer's introduction and footnotes are helpful for putting it in context.

MacMorgan, Kaatryn. *Wicca 333: Advanced Topics in Wiccan Belief.* **Lincoln, NE: iUniverse, 2003.**

If you're looking for a book that is absolutely beyond the Wicca 101 titles, this is it. Writing from an eclectic perspective, MacMorgan asks readers to consider Wiccan theology, history, and magical practice with a degree of seriousness rarely found in books about Witchcraft of any kind. We're not in agreement about every issue—and that's not the point, of course—but this book was a game-changer for me as a young Witch and is one that I often use in teaching today.

Mankey, Jason. *Transformative Witchcraft: The Greater Mysteries.* **Woodbury, MN: Llewellyn Publications, 2019.**

Mankey discuses some of modern Witchcraft's most mysterious rites and rituals, including drawing down the moon, the Great Rite, raising the cone of power, and initiation. In other books, these are often described only in passing, or not at all, leaving the reader wondering how to actually explore them and work them effectively. With his trademark good humor and characteristically thorough research, Mankey's book is indispensable for Witches of all types and is absolutely mandatory for Wiccan Witches.

McGuire, Meredith B. *Lived Religion: Faith and Practice in Everyday Life.* **New York: Oxford University Press, 2008.**

We often talk about religion as though it's a monolith, but the truth is that there's an impossible amount of variety in how people practice. What's more, a lot of that variety occurs between how religions exist within their formal structures and doctrines versus how people actually experience them on the ground. Read this book to expand your understanding of what religion is and how it can work.

O'Brien, Lora. *A Practical Guide to Pagan Priesthood: Community Leadership and Vocation.* **Woodbury, MN: Llewellyn Publications, 2019.**

Because our traditions are decentralized and tend to defy structures typical of other religions, Pagan leaders tend to be self-taught, self-directed, and lacking in a lot of the support that makes this such a difficult vocation. In this book, O'Brien takes a broad and thorough approach to providing that support. What does it mean to be a priest? How does one serve others, and why? How does one negotiate relationships with deities, deal with tricky group dynamics, maintain personal boundaries, and engage in outreach? O'Brien deftly tackles these and many more. Whether or not you identify as Pagan or as a member of a priesthood, this is a must read for Witches in positions of leadership.

Rauls, Venecia. *The Second Circle: Tools for the Advancing Pagan.* **New York: Citadel Press, 2004.**

There aren't many books out there specifically for Pagans seeking mastery, well past the beginner stage but in need of guidance as to where to go next. This is one of them! Witches who have been trained in formal covens may already have these ideas and techniques in their arsenal, but for those who've relied on books or social media, this is a worthwhile resource.

Sylvan, Dianne. *The Circle Within: Creating a Wiccan Spiritual Tradition.* **St. Paul, MN: Llewellyn, 2003.**

This has long been a cherished title for practitioners who are looking for something more in their experience of Wicca. Sylvan guides readers in creating a deeper, more meaningful, highly personal relationship with both the gods of Wicca, and its core traditions and beliefs. This short book is sure to please Wiccans at all levels, but may also provide some insight into daily practice for other types of Witches as well.

Williams, Brandy. *For the Love of the Gods: The History and Modern Practice of Theurgy.* **Woodbury, MN: Llewellyn Publications, 2016.**

How does one go about actually working with gods? Williams answers this question, both from the perspective of historical Paganism—from Egypt, Greece, and beyond—and from today's contemporary Pagan teachers and scholars. A broad, challenging work, this book is appropriate for polytheistic Witches who are interested in deepening their own relationships with their gods (or forging new ones).

Wulf, Andrea. *The Invention of Nature: Alexander von Humboldt's New World.* **New York: Vintage Books, 2015.**

Do not make the mistake of thinking that this is a mere biography! As fascinating as German naturalist Alexander von Humboldt is, this book made the suggested reading list because it is a valuable account of how our modern understanding of "nature" came to be, as well as how this evolved into the environmentalism movement. As Witches, we sometimes assume that our core values are ancient and essential, but nature, it turns out, is actually quite modern.

Notes

Notes

Notes